Don't Give Up, Don't Give In

Curtis L. Ivery

Library of Congress Cataloging-in-Publication Data
available upon request

Published in the United States by Beaufort Books
www.BeaufortBooks.com

Distributed by Midpoint Trade Books
www.MidpointTrade.com

This edition ISBN: 9780825307898

Printed in the United States of America

Don't Give Up, Give Up, Don't Give In

Curtis L. Ivery

BEAUFORT
BOOKS

ACKNOWLEDGMENT

This book is a labor of love and respect, both given and received. My love and respect for my family, community and culture, and especially for the many young men who need a guiding hand. I have also been the recipient of love and respect from so many who have helped support and guide me in this process. I thank my loving wife, Ola, my son Marcus and his family, and my daughter Angela and hers. Without question, my love and gratitude goes to my grandchildren, who serve as an endless light for me, serving as inspiration and a bright guiding light. To my friends, colleagues, mentors and mentees, I also thank them for who they are and all that they do to make a difference in the lives of others.

CONTENTS

FOREWORD

One of the most important skills that any leader develops early in life is to be silent, and to listen. In listening you can develop fresh insights and ideas for positive action. In listening you can rescue and uplift voices that are often marginalized.

But first, you will do this to hear and understand your own voice, and to stay grounded in a sometimes chaotic and disruptive world. Later, you'll use that skill to build confidence in cutting through both the noise and bluster to discover who others are, and appreciate their diversity of perspectives. People do, after all, tell you who they are. You simply need to believe them.

This simple but profound lesson runs through the book *Don't Give Up, Don't Give In*, and with good reason.

Like an experienced surgeon performing on our maladies, Dr. Curtis L. Ivery, writes from the perspective of a lifelong advocate for young people and for equal access to higher education and the opportunities that it provides. He understands young people and in this book is tapping into something that many of them already know: They have a voice that needs to be heard. Teaching them how to use it is the transformational project of this book.

In other words the book could also be titled "Who Will Speak for Me?" because Dr. Ivery in this literary masterpiece is speaking rightly to the heart and minds of many young people who are struggling to build self-esteem.

Understanding and knowing how to use your unique voice is the critical foundation that allows you to take risks without allowing them to take you out; to explore without getting lost; and to counter those voices from friends, peers, your neighborhood, popular culture and mass media that insist your voice isn't valuable, isn't important and isn't vital to your future and, to theirs.

Knowing and appreciating your identity, your voice, is what will build an unflinching sense that you matter; that you are important, and deserve happiness, opportunity and the chance to experience the world in ways that feed your soul and the life of your community.

Listening to young people, and teaching them to understand how important developing their own inner voice has to be at the heart of our efforts to help them grow into whole, well-rounded adults. Our young people have talent, creativity, insight and capacity beyond imagination.

Despite this, they are often afraid that their ideas, talent and abilities will be dismissed as unpractical or silly. They've been lectured to, told what they should be concentrating on, or told that they need to fit someone else's template to be "successful." Success is not measured in what glitters but rather the ability to make a meaningful impact both on individuals and in society.

Dr. Ivery understands this. His life work is the definition of meaningful impact. He doesn't lecture. With hard-earned wisdom, he encourages young men to take pride in the knowledge that their lives and minds have tremendous value. It's by treating both mind and body with respect that you truly soar, Dr. Ivery teaches, and become the best version of yourself.

That's a lesson worth learning, and passing on to the next generation. This book also echoes the calls of leaders and thinkers of recent history whose work reflected the need to prepare the next generation of leaders. Trendsetters like Dr. Benjamin E. Mays, the former president of Morehouse College and mentor to Dr. Martin Luther King Jr., Maya Angelou and others used the creative force of their intellect to challenge all of us to develop and build strong leaders of tomorrow.

In *Don't Give Up, Don't Give In,* Dr. Ivery also renders a monumental contribution in addressing the complex crisis facing today's youth. This book is a resplendent addition to a world in need of strategies, ideas and commitment to better prepare and equip our youth for the challenges and complexities of their time.

A strongly recommended reading, this book is a lasting tribute to the power of an educated understanding of the needs facing our young people.

Bankole Thompson
Op-Ed Columnist
The Detroit News

INTRODUCTION

Say there, young man: Do you ever stop to think about what you're going to do with your life? Are you ever bothered when your buddies give you a hard time about something you don't want to do? What about girls? Do you understand what they really want, how they think or how they should be treated?

Believe it or not, I've been where you are right now. Yes, everyone was young once — even people my age. I'm what some would call an old timer. I was around before cell phones, iPads and video games. But, some things never change, including drugs, gangs, algebra and locker room talk about sex. And no matter how much time passes, we still experience the same worries about money, success, teachers we can't get along with and bullies who try to make life miserable.

In this book, we're going to talk about all of them. Man to man. That means me and you — the tough guy with the scowl on his face. It means you with the swagger and you, the kid with all the books stuffed into your backpack. It means you with the sagging jeans and you, the one packing for college. It also includes you on the basketball court hoopin' with hopes of blazing a trail all the way to the NBA.

I'm talking to each and every one of you — in my own language and in the way I see fit. Yes, I'm old-fashioned. I'm an elder with two grandsons who call me Papa. But, that's one of the reasons our talks are going to be so useful. Each chapter is going to address a different topic that I believe you would like to discuss. Chances are I've already wandered along the paths you're now traveling. I've had my share of victories and mistakes. Sometimes, I made my parents proud; other times, not so proud. I've been where you are. But, I always dusted myself off and kept going. My journey through highs and lows eventually led to my share of accomplishments — all because I never gave up. The same power is within you. When I was your age, I imagined an exciting future. Now, I want to help you imagine and live one too.

Whether you realize it or not, we all could use a boost now and then. Think of me as an experienced old friend with a lot of down-home, tried-and-true, hard-knock lessons. I want you to benefit from what I have done (or not) before you. I want these lessons to be your conscience, mentor and guide, as both my parents were for me, because I care deeply about so many boys growing up today without the guidance they need. Read my words carefully and do just as the title of this book suggests: *Build your life* into the best future you can imagine for yourself.

CHAPTER 1

MANHOOD: IT'S A TRIP

"You can't measure manhood with a tape line around his biceps."
— Billy Sunday

Has anyone ever told you to "man up?" Were you annoyed or simply amused? Did you change your attitude and agree to do whatever was expected, or ignore it and keep doing as you were before? To be a real man, you have to first be honest with yourself. You must assess your own talents and shortcomings, develop unbreakable self-confidence, and have a ferocious hunger to succeed.

Take it from an old warrior — not the military type, but someone with a few battle scars from years spent overcoming challenges and creating victories. I plunged into the same scary new world of manhood you are about to enter. When I was your age, I had a few fears about the future, too. Don't get me wrong. I was a big, strong guy who played basketball and football. But all the while, I was privately terrified of growing up. I knew that one day I was going to be a man and that meant being responsible for an entire family, paying bills and taking care of serious grownup business. A wife and children were going to turn to me, depend on me and expect me to have the answers. The prospect and mystery of it all can be pretty intimidating to any young person.

When you become a man, you become the provider and protector. I was looking forward to it, but at the same time, didn't feel quite prepared. So, I found myself wondering and fretting. I know you can feel me on this subject. I'm sure you get it. Being a man means you must first shed whatever phobias and anxieties you have about life.

Even as a little boy, you probably realized that you shouldn't be afraid of anything for too long, not even the dark. Males know instinctively that one day we will have to guide our wives and children through the darkness as well as the light. We are the hunters expected to perform bold feats. Yet, we're not always convinced that we've been taught how to handle these responsibilities.

That's why it's important to start thinking about inner strength, determination and masculinity — especially if you're preparing to graduate. It's both liberating and frightening to walk across that stage, get a diploma and be told to go out into the world now and make things happen. It's an enormous leap when it's suddenly all on you. Many can mess up now and then and go back home for a while to get it all together again. But, that fallback is not an option for everyone. Instead of being supported through young adulthood, they're told over and over to simply "man up," which, of course, can lead to confusion and frustration. Is "man up" just an expression? What does it imply? What does it really take to be a man?

Let's start with the fact that you're not quite there yet. You are *almost* a man — coming of age, which means you are at an in-between stage of life. Your rites of passage through this period are the new situations you face, the major decisions you make and the baby steps you take into the vibrant new arena of grown folks. You will stumble. You might even trip and fall. When you lose your way, reach out for the steadying hand of older folks like me. Then get up and keep moving.

Right now, you should be doing the groundwork by developing a value system. You should be making decisions about what you want to do with your life and planning how to achieve this goal. Map it out. Literally create a chart listing each step. Four guideposts could point you in the right direction. Make note of them, preferably on paper, but at least in your mind.

GUIDEPOST 1: LATCH ON TO A POSITIVE MENTOR

Be it your dad, granddad, an uncle, teacher or church member, find someone special you've admired or a man in the community you really respect for all the right reasons. Make sure he is the right type of person for your journey, and then make him your role model.

Here's a more personal example of what I mean: I grew up in a modest little area in Amarillo, Texas. There weren't many successful people in my neighborhood who were what you would call "well off." But, there was this one brother who always drove a brand new Cadillac in the company of beautiful women. It would have been too easy to make him a hero and decide that's who I wanted to imitate. For a while, in fact, I thought he really was "the man" — until discovering that he was actually a hustler. I made a conscious choice at that point not to focus on him, his car or his women anymore, but to look elsewhere for someone who would inspire and fill me with pride.

I eventually got to know this really popular teacher at school. All the kids liked him. He was a cool dresser and had a very pretty wife. Instantly, he became my champion. I hung around after school just to ask questions. I listened to the way he talked, observed how he carried himself and interacted with others. He proved that good guys had great things, personified my idea of a success and served as an example of the kind of man I wanted to be.

I understood at the same time that I had to invent myself and mold my future. This teacher probably didn't even realize I was patterning myself after him. The person you latch on to doesn't have to know that either. All that matters is that you find a positive individual to look up to, someone who gives you a reason to believe that you can make your dreams come true. If he is someone you can talk to, even better. Ask him what life was like when he was younger. What kinds of friends did he have? Was he rich or poor? How did he get past struggles at home or school? What and who kept him motivated?

Everyone gets blasted with problems from time to time, but not everyone knows how to handle them. Your role model should be someone who beat any odds stacked up against him. How did he do it? Listen carefully to what he has to say and the right path should become much easier to find.

GUIDEPOST 2: WORK HARD

Make up your mind that no one can or will work as long or with as much effort and enthusiasm as you. When I started college, I couldn't help but notice that more than a few kids were finishing exams before me. While I was still hunched over my desk, they were getting up and leaving. I was struggling and they were walking out the door with As and Bs.

I was a pretty good student who took pride in my work. Yet, I wasn't doing as well as I felt I could or should. Somehow, some way, I needed to figure out how to improve. Eventually, I approached one of my honor-student friends and asked how much time he devoted to studying. Without hesitation, he replied, "two hours a night." I thanked him and immediately went to work. From that point on, I studied four hours a night, figuring that if two hours led to good grades, four would lead to excellence. My idea worked. My grades shot up and I, too, started acing exams with ease.

I even created a new personal motto: "If you walk two miles, I'll walk four." If others are working hard, work harder. If they're working harder, then guess what? You should step up your game, too. Most high-achievers get there by making up their minds to go the extra mile and do more than anyone else. It doesn't matter if they're running a 300-yard dash in the Olympics or trying to become the best algebra student in the 11th grade. Whatever the goal, they all made the same decision I made years ago. They found out how long others practice and they doubled it. To go farther, you must go harder.

It's a simple, wonderful, proven method of success for many you probably already admire, including superstar actor Will Smith. In an interview that's been widely viewed on the Internet, Smith describes himself as an ordinary guy who got ahead more than anything because he refused to give up.

"The only thing that I see that is distinctly different about me is I'm not afraid to die on a treadmill," he said. "I will not be out-worked, period. You might have more talent than me, you might be smarter than me, you might be sexier than me, and you might be all of those things you got on me in nine categories. But, if we get on the treadmill together, there are two things: You're getting off first, or I'm going to die. It's really that simple, right?

"You're not going to out-work me. It's such a simple, basic concept. The guy who is willing to hustle the most is going to be the guy that just gets that loose ball… I say all the time if you stay ready, you ain't gotta get ready."

GUIDEPOST 3: IT'S OK TO PRETEND

If you want courage, pretend to have as much as necessary. Just act mentally tough enough for any challenge. Are you juggling school and a job? No problem for a man with imagination. Moving from middle to high school? Act brave and soon enough, you'll be brave. Facing a job you're afraid you won't be able to do? Keep telling yourself you can handle it and you will. The mind dictates more of your reality than you know.

In the old days we used to say, "Fake it until you make it." It's not about deceiving anyone, but taking a giant first step toward becoming a man. By foreseeing results in your mind, you gain confidence, set goals and think big. Coupled with a solid work ethic, mental visualization can make you unstoppable. Top athletes do it as a regular part of their training because they know they must visualize desired results even while physically preparing for them. There is power in the imagination. For example, when my son was eight, my wife and I heard someone singing exceptionally well on the radio in another room and wondered who it was. When we asked if he knew, we were shocked to learn it was him.

"How did you do that?" we asked, puzzled.

"It was easy," he answered. "All I did was listen to the radio and pretend that I was the guy singing the song."

He didn't become an entertainer, wasn't interested. Yet, my wife and I were impressed that child's play could result in such a beautiful sound. What stunning make-believe are you nourishing? Do you want to be the kind of man others admire? Do you want to be a politician? How about an accountant? Police officer or artist? Then believe you are on the job right now. Pretend. Conjure up an image in your mind and hold it there. Your faith will take you far if you allow it to. Remember, you have dreams for a reason. Don't ignore them. All you have to do is hold on to your most cherished visions and believe.

GUIDEPOST 4: SAFEGUARD YOUR MIND

By the age of 18, you will have witnessed more than 200,000 incidents of mock violence and maybe even a few real ones. They occur constantly on television, in the movies and in video games. Now before you roll your eyes and start thinking, "Oh no, here we go again," hear me out.

You're a male — the alpha dog. It's natural to be aggressive at times and feel the need to show off your physical strength. To rise above the animal kingdom, however, those tendencies must be tempered with discipline and constraint.

When I was in high school, I took it upon myself to protect one of my close friends. Other kids at school knew about his learning disability and a few tried to take advantage of it. Sometimes, he would go all day without eating because a bully had stolen his lunch. I would be furious, a fierce guardian of my vulnerable friend, looking for anyone who had hurt his feelings or harmed him in any way. We're wired to defend, protect, prove ourselves, seek adventure and stand up as the men of our households. But, there's a big difference between asserting yourself on those grounds and stuffing your consciousness with dehumanizing images of brutal violence.

The old saying, "Garbage in, garbage out," means simply that what you put into a container is exactly what you'll get out. In this case, the container is your mind and you need to protect it just like you would protect anything you cherish. No one would put Kool-Aid in the gas tank of their car if they expect to drive anywhere. So, why fill your head with negative music and videos and still expect to move in a positive direction? Your mind can only take you where your thoughts lead. They are the fuel that propels your life forward. What kind of fuel are you pouring into your mind's tank? Are you filling it with Kool-Aid or high-powered octane?

Do your thoughts wander down a road paved with violent images and negative messages? If so, toss in a few uplifting scenes and words. In order to become a man of purpose — a man who could run a business, make a good husband and father — you have to take the time to build the right qualities in your mind and spirit.

Cultivate your inner being by taking in ideas that will help you create the future you deserve. Look for empowering quotes and inspirational messages to carry in your wallet or tape to your bathroom mirror. Make friends with guys at school who have something interesting and positive to talk about. Watch entertaining TV programs that teach about history, science, the arts or nature. Listen to music that lifts the spirit rather than dragging it into the gutter. Read material that offers life skills.

Look for movies about men who have an amazing influence on the lives of others. They might include Martin Luther King, Jr., Nelson Mandela, Sidney Poitier, Tom Hanks or Forest Whittaker. Well-known humanitarians such as Blair Underwood, Brad Pitt and Sean Penn could be added to the list. Take your pick. Learn about them to mimic their admirable ways and habits. When you read stories or view films about people who have had a favorable impact on society, you become more motivated to do the same. You develop a thirst for more knowledge. School will become fun and your goals won't seem nearly so far away.

You'll also find that greatness doesn't happen overnight. You have to work at it like everything else. As you do, the idea of reaching the finish line — becoming a good parent, the breadwinner and future leader — gradually seems more realistic. And I can promise you something else: You won't get annoyed next time you're hit with those two little words, "man up." In fact, you may never hear that challenge again — unless, of course, it's from your own lips for the benefit of some other young man.

CHAPTER 2

BUILD IT, LIVE IN IT

"Character cannot be developed in ease and quiet. Only through experience of trial and suffering can the soul be strengthened, ambition inspired, and success achieved."

— Helen Keller

Years ago, I heard a clever story about a prominent businessman who hired a young neighbor to help with yard work. The older guy took a special interest in the neighbor. In addition to various work projects, he began to mentor and offer him guidance.

One day, he made a suggestion that the young man never expected: He asked him to build a house. He said he would be out of the country for the year. During his absence, he expected his employee/mentee to buy everything necessary to assemble the home they had discussed. He left him a check for a substantial amount of money and told him to buy whatever he needed.

A year passed and the businessman returned. The first thing he did was visit the young man to ask about the project.

"Well," he inquired, "did you build the house?"

"Yes," replied the young man.

"Okay," the businessman said, looking quite pleased. "Did you build a good foundation?"

"I did."

"Then tell me, did you use the right materials?" the businessman asked.

"Yes," the neighbor replied.

"Well what about concrete? Did you use the cement and lumber I left?" Again, the answer was yes.

"Did you install storm windows and make sure all the paneling was secure?"

"Yes sir."

"Did you use the proper wood and nails?"

When the young man answered in the affirmative yet again, he received the greatest surprise of his life: a shiny new key.

"This is your house," he was told with a smile. "It's yours to live in for the rest of your life."

The moral of that story is simple. You only get out of life what you put into it. Everything you do is part of the foundation you are building for the future. Many people, especially teenagers, don't realize that the decisions they make today lead to the circumstances, opportunities, pains and joys of tomorrow. Your grades determine the kind of job you eventually will get. Your job will determine how much money you have, which then determines where and how you live and even what school your children will attend.

Your future will grow from the actions you are taking right now. What are you planting? Are you sowing negative seeds of anger and self-doubt? Are you planting impatience, laziness and disrespect for authority? If so, you could be filling the soil of your future with hardships. Your stubborn ways will come back to haunt you in the form of missed opportunities and bad habits so embedded they become difficult or nearly impossible to break.

On the other hand, if you are setting goals, cultivating skills and planting positive seeds of self-control, you can expect a future that includes college, a chance to travel, an array of talents and the home and life of your dreams. That's because you started building it when you were young and able.

You will become the composite of the experiences in your life. You can make it a good composite or bad. Everything we do becomes the bed we make and the house we live in. All deeds come back into our lives in some way. That's often referred to as "what goes around comes around," and it's something you're feeding into even when you don't know it at this stage in your life.

Whether you're 12, 14 or 17 years old, you need to ask yourself: "How do I want to be remembered? What kind of person do I want to become?" To find the answer, try assisting someone else in need. When you do, you'll feel so good you'll want to do it again. Helping others will then become a natural part of who you are — seeds that will produce good things for you. You can't wait until you're 40 years old to try and change. It's not going to work that way. This is real, one-time only and for keeps. It's not a play, and there is no dress rehearsal.

I found that out my first year in high school. A friend who played on the football team with me met with an unfortunate fate that I happened to witness. His name was Michael, and I have never forgotten him.

During a school dance at the YMCA, one of the rough kids got into a shoving match with Michael. No one took it as seriously then as they might now because guns weren't the norm in my day. But, somehow this guy managed to get his hands on one. He shot Michael, stunning everyone in the hall, but none more than me. I was in a big fog, it seemed so unreal. Michael turned to run. I followed and said, "Michael you're going to be okay." But, there was blood coming out of his nose and I didn't know what to do. I'd seen similar scenes on TV, but this was just too shocking to comprehend. When I learned that my friend had died, I don't think I really got it at first. I didn't understand the finality of death. I was out of it for a long time and was quite fearful, although I wasn't sure of what.

I grew up after that incident. You cannot have an experience like that and not instantly be changed. Suddenly, overnight, I had an understanding of cause and effect and the connection between what would happen if A and B occurred. I also realized then that I needed to make decisions about the people I wanted and allowed around me. I knew I couldn't let situations or circumstances define me. I realized I had to know where I was going because "aimless" was not a destination.

I also recognized that I was going to have to fend for myself one day. I consciously began building and shaping the person I wanted to be. As I worked through my pain, I started to understand that rules exist for our protection. Many of my peers didn't understand that and I'm pretty sure a lot of your friends don't get it either. But when I lost my best friend to senseless violence, I learned the importance of all rules and obeying them.

I also began to focus on another major concern of adolescence: self-control. Do you know how to count to three and quiet your temper before you melt down, strike out or fatally wound someone? Self-control means you are the captain governing all the urges and desires surging through your mind and body. It means not acting on every whim or impulse, but stopping yourself from saying or doing things that could be quite damaging and irreversible.

Bullets are devastating, but words can also be a weapon with serious consequences. If you have ever spread or been the victim of false gossip, you realize that the effects can outlast the real truth for a lifetime. Anyone who has been subjected to gossip, name-calling and nasty comments knows how long it takes for those injuries to heal.

In your effort to build a house sturdy enough to weather the storm of life, make sure you use the plain, old-fashioned but dependable bricks of common sense — including the one we've all heard for good reason about choosing your words carefully.

They can be hurtful and inflammatory, and once spoken can't be taken back.

We are all powerful beings who must learn how to use that power wisely by struggling with it at some point in our lives. My peers and I used to wrestle with what we wanted to be, while privately admitting we wanted more but didn't know what direction to take. Most of us thought the military was the answer because we didn't see many college grads around us, so we were at a loss as to other choices. Fortunately, our parents taught us morals, ethics, fairness and the importance of loving others. My mother always said, "If you love people, you'll be okay."

Her words ring true to this day. But, you need more than that to shape and structure the house of "you." You're going to need determination, too. In other words, finish what you start.

When my eighth grade basketball coach put me on the sidelines, I quit the team. Now I realize that I didn't handle that situation very well. The coach didn't let me play and I overreacted by taking myself out of the game. This decision led to disappointment and regret for no one but me. I get it now. I needed to let the coach determine when I was ready. Like everyone on any team, I wanted to be a starting player. But, I couldn't — not because of the coach, but because I wasn't patient enough to let him prepare me for the next stage.

I never forgave myself for that. I didn't get to play middle school basketball, even though I knew I had the talent. But, the screw-up was all mine and mine alone. I'm the one who yanked the bricks out of that room in my house. I didn't give myself a chance to win. I just took myself out of the race.

There's actually a term for this: "stick-to-it-iveness." It's a crazy word that sums up an important attitude. It means hanging in there even when it gets tough. When you do, you are so proud of yourself later, especially when the opportunities begin to fall at your feet as a result. Doors will open all because of a skill you developed from doing something that once seemed too hard or impossible.

Does it feel like I'm pushing you? You bet I am. I'm telling you to actively cultivate the skills you would like to master. Make a list of your goals and how you're going to meet them. Write down your positive qualities and put stars next to them, then add your negative traits and make a note about how you're going to overcome those before they overcome you. Here are a few more building tips:

• Look in the mirror every day and tell yourself: *I am powerful. I can do and be whatever I want.*

• Read your list of goals at least once a week.

• Clip a couple of inspiring images from magazines. Find pictures that really motivate you to move toward a positive future. Tape them to your mirror, dresser or school locker, or in a loose leaf book.

• Jot down the traits and habits of the most successful people you know or have heard about. Don't compare yourself to them in discouraging terms of what you're not, but always look for positive characteristics you can emulate to improve yourself.

• Is there anyone in your life pulling you down? Promise yourself to stop associating with such people.

- What good deeds have you performed lately? Have you cut the grass for an elderly neighbor or helped your mom out at home? Think of something kind you can do and then do it.

- Never, ever give up — ever.

Build your future by building yourself. You can create a new you, a better you, one thought at a time. Not everyone knows this, but thoughts have a lot of impact on the kind of life we lead. To create that amazing world you're hoping for, you have to hold on to the thought that it is indeed possible. Flip through magazines, search college catalogues and look online for examples of your heart's desires. You can create your own reality and map out your future by steering your mind toward the things you want to make happen. Your actions will follow.

Does that sound like fun? It is, but it involves a lot of work as well. Life will never be easy. There are no shortcuts. If you do something well, it's probably because you worked at it.

Start now. Don't let fear prevent you from reaching high. It's not only unproductive, but often irrational. We fear that we're not going to be able to make the track team or do well in certain classes. We worry about not being cool enough, "down" enough or the man who everyone wants to follow. But, when we apply ourselves, failure rarely happens. We usually do make the cut or earn a decent grade. And even if we're not "the man," we still have our share of friends who will think we're pretty cool.

There are some seriously justifiable fears, though — drugs, gangs and the violence that is so rampant today. Our worries used to be much different. While we may have faced the challenges of integration and civil rights, we didn't fear being out in our own neighborhoods or playing football in the street after dark. Drugs weren't nearly as widespread then; most of us never even heard about marijuana until we started college.

For you, these worries are everywhere, but you don't have to let them overwhelm you. Find the right crowd — that unique group of kids you relate to best. Carve out your niche and establish yourself as the chess champ. Even a nerd gets a little honor if he has a title. Earn and embrace your position as the honor-roll geek who doesn't care what anyone says about "schoolboys." Be student council president, editor of the yearbook or the hot running back on the football team. Everyone can do something.

Whatever your thing is, do it well and claim your honors. You get respect that way and more credibility among those who matter most.

While you're at it, stay clear of troublemakers; they're nothing but bad for themselves and you. Get so involved in school clubs and extracurricular activities so that you're not in the wrong place at the wrong time. Another benefit: Bullies can't find you because, with your hectic schedule, you're never around.

As for drugs, there's only one rule that works: Always avoid them unless prescribed by a doctor. Old fogeys like me might all sound the same, but it's because we are firsthand witnesses to the importance of a clear, healthy mind. Don't get started and you'll never miss or regret it. Remember, you are building your house. The actions you take now will become the foundation of a powerful and magnificent structure or a raggedy little shack. Which will it be?

CHAPTER 3

ATTITUDE IS EVERYTHING

"I never had much patience with the multitudes of people who are always ready to explain why one cannot succeed. I have always had high regard for the man who could tell me how to succeed."
— Booker T. Washington

"Attitude is everything." That simple statement sums up all you need to know about getting ahead and reaching your dreams. It's an easy lesson that can be learned from a number of individuals, including a funny-faced, floppy-eared critter created by Looney Tunes — Bugs Bunny. I'm not kidding. The carrot-chomping cartoon character actually has something more powerful to say than, "What's up, Doc?"

Think about it. Bugs is clever and comes up with ingenious ways to get out of tricky situations. He has the confidence to laugh in the face of problems and the strength to stand up to his enemies.

He has the courage to look danger right in the eye and keep bouncing along no matter what villain is chasing him or obstacle is in his way. Now, that's what I call a good attitude. If it makes sense for a "wascally wabbit" like him, it can most certainly work for a more serious young man like you.

Evaluate your own attitude. Are you generally agreeable and cooperative? Do you listen to your parents and teachers? Do you keep trying after you have failed? If you honestly answer no to any of these questions, it's time to work on your perspective. Start by taking a few basic actions. They are:

TAKE PRIDE IN YOUR WORK

Do your personal best. Your quality of work is like your calling card. It makes a statement about you and sells your skills to others. Any job that is sloppily done suggests a poor work ethic, low self-esteem and laziness. If it's halfway done, it shows you don't finish your work or take it seriously. But, a job well done tells the world that you believe in yourself and will go the extra mile. It implies you can be trusted, live up to your potential and aspire to excellence.

As a young boy, I remember going out into the backyard with my dad to help cut tree limbs. I started to feel bad because I noticed he had cut several enormous limbs in a short time, while I had only taken down a couple that were pretty skimpy. When I said something about it, he smiled and replied, "Son, don't do my best. Your job is to do your best." Good attitudes are born when you decide not to quit until doing all you can.

The Rev. Martin Luther King, Jr. is well known for his passionate message about giving your all even to the lowest-paying job. He said: "If a man is called to be a street sweeper, he should sweep streets even as a Michelangelo painted, or Beethoven composed music or Shakespeare wrote poetry. He should sweep streets so well that all the hosts of heaven and earth will pause to say, 'Here lived a great street sweeper who did his job well.'"

BE RESPECTFUL

You don't have to agree with everyone, nor do you have to share the same interests or ideas as those around you. You don't even have to like them. However, you must respect everyone — children, your peers and adults. Listen patiently as a matter of basic courtesy. You may be bored, but it's rude to yawn in someone's face. It's one thing to share your ideas, but quite another to put others down for not seeing the world as you do. Present your views calmly and politely, and give others an opportunity to express themselves as well. And don't get bent out of shape every time someone tells you to do something you don't want to do. It could be that your parents are right about curfew or limiting your time with certain friends. The teacher who is always yapping in your ear may well be trying to steer you toward a place that could change your life.

BE CONSIDERATE

Young men with good attitudes look out for others. They think before they speak to ensure their words aren't hurtful. They are polite. They don't push and shove to be first in line. They open doors for women and continue to hold them open when they see an elderly person approaching or someone younger struggling with a heavy package. They might even offer to carry that package, or simply wait to make sure the person gets to his or her car safely. Having a good attitude means being aware that others have feelings, concerns and needs too. You're not the only one capable of a bad day or foul mood, but often are the only one in a position to lift the gloom for someone else with the easy kindness of a greeting or helping hand.

MAKE A PLAN

It has been said that the journey of a thousand miles begins with a single step. A young man with a good attitude takes responsibility for that journey. Know where you want to go, do what it takes to get there. Create an internal map and keep moving toward your destination, step by step. Take the classes you need. Make the required sacrifices. Get off the phone and study, even when you'd much rather be talking. Pass up a chance to go to a movie now and then to do something more constructive. Instead of shooting hoops one Saturday, put extra hours into your job, schoolwork or building a special relationship.

It's all about investing in yourself and your future. A guy with a bad attitude is one who doesn't make an effort, but expects good results anyway because he doesn't understand how nothing from nothing leaves nothing. Just as you can't take anything out of the bank if you never make deposits, life only gives what we put into it. When things aren't going your way, don't get an attitude. Instead, make a plan.

LEARN TO LISTEN

Really hearing what others are saying is a skill some people never develop. As a result, they fumble through mistake after mistake because they don't completely tune-in in the first place. To be a good listener, you must clear your mind of distractions —

including, most importantly, your own thoughts for a moment — to be receptive to what the speaker is trying to tell you. Too many young men suddenly flip their minds off like a light switch or let their thoughts wander. Your coach might be explaining a new strategy and you're daydreaming about an evening with your girlfriend. This is not only a bad habit; it's the sign of a bad attitude. Those with good listening skills have fewer problems because they don't zone out when important information is being shared. Focus.

PAY YOUR DUES

When trying to accomplish something new in life, we all have to crawl or stumble and sometimes fall in the beginning. Instead of learning to ski by plunging down a huge mountain, you start out on a big mound of snow known as the bunny hill. You pay your dues by practicing and falling where it doesn't hurt so much before boarding a ski lift and heading for the big slopes.

Learning a language or anything else requires the same patience. You don't start with complex phrases like "Tengo un dolor de cabeza que horrible" (I have a horrible headache), but with small words used before short sentences like "Como esta usted?" (How are you?). You listen to recordings, perform drills and repeat phrases over and over to get the right accent and pronunciation before impressing anyone with your conversational skills.

Young men with positive attitudes aren't afraid to begin at the beginning. They gladly take menial jobs washing cars or cleaning toilets because that's the best they can do at the moment, knowing it's just a start and nothing permanent.

Never be too proud to roll up your sleeves and sweep floors, shovel snow or pull weeds if that's what it takes. Little tasks can grow into part-time jobs that eventually bloom into full time. This land of opportunity abounds with true stories of people who started at the very bottom and, with nothing more than perseverance and attitude, made it all the way to the very top.

OPEN YOUR MIND

Close your mind and you might as well throw away the key, too. Know-it-alls don't believe that anyone else can teach them anything. I have many years and accomplishments behind me, but continue to learn new things all the time. If smart people four times your age are still learning, it's safe to assume that you don't yet know it all either. Knowledge is timeless and endless. It provides the seeds, water, and sunlight that help us grow. And when we stop growing, opportunities die.

THE WORLD DOESN'T OWE YOU ANYTHING

The preceding steps are clear explanations of what you need to do to get where you want to go. If you choose not to prepare, go to school, study and work hard, don't get mad at life for not giving you anything good in return. But, earn it and you shall receive it. You are your own masterpiece. View yourself as a shapeless lump of clay and ask: "What will I make of myself today? What will I do today to move me closer to my dream?" Then do it.

A good attitude is better than any talent or intelligence. You can be talented, but if your attitude is in the wrong place you'll walk — or be pushed — away from opportunity. You could be the smartest kid in school, but that doesn't mean a thing if you're not smart enough to prove it in the appropriate time and place.

You are one of 7 billion people on the planet. In what seems like an infinite world, you must be mindful of two things: You matter and so do others. You are a unique, one-of-a-kind individual who gets to roam around this planet either helping others or kicking them around. You can be a liar or wear your word like a badge of honor. You can be kind or mean. You can take responsibility for all your actions or blame everyone else.

If you choose integrity, compassion and self-respect, it will take you from poor to rich in every way imaginable. It will transform you from loser to winner, from someone with self-doubt to one who makes things happen because, as exemplified by our tenaciously upbeat friend Bugs at the beginning of this chapter, attitude is indeed everything.

CHAPTER

WHAT'S SO COOL ABOUT BEING ANGRY?

"The fighter is never angry."
— Lao Tzu

Picture this: Damon and R.J. are hanging together, listening to music in a neighborhood park. A few more young men show up and, before long, they are laughing loudly, teasing one another and talking smack. Damon says something funny about R.J.'s girlfriend. Everyone cracks up — everyone, that is, but R.J., who instantly flushes with anger and takes a swing at Damon. He curses him out, even threatens to go get a weapon.

Damon tries to apologize, but it doesn't matter. R.J. has no interest in controlling himself or listening to reason. He thinks it is normal — even cool — to get angry because that's mostly what he's seen around him all his life. He mistakenly thinks it makes him seem tough. The angrier and more menacing he is, the

37

more he feels like a man. No one has taught him that a real man is the master of his emotions. A real man knows that unchecked rage drives people to do things they otherwise wouldn't or shouldn't do.

Unfortunately, no one has ever warned R.J. about the destructive power of this ugly thing known as losing your temper. No one has shown him how to turn the negative force into something else by pausing to refocus. As quickly as you might say or do something you regret for the rest of your life, you can picture yourself on the basketball court just having fun again. You can just as easily make a comment that lightens the mood so everyone moves on. At the very least, take a moment to consider the negative consequences of failing to control your angry feelings. Be the real man who backs down first if that's what it takes to safely defuse a dangerous situation.

Use all that energy later to lift weights, do some pushups, or head to the basketball court to unleash your wrath in the form of harmless hard play. Blocking out anger will still come in handy when it's time to hit the books. While studying, you'll be so busy tuning out the situation that made you mad earlier, you'll find it easier to concentrate on the words in front of you. Your anger will be the fuel to keep you focused on what you are really trying to learn.

Anger is nothing more than misplaced energy raging out of control like wildfire. Your heartbeat speeds up, your body turns hot and the thoughts tearing through your brain get muddled. It's called "not thinking straight" for a good reason. If you allow those feelings to dominate, they will consume your logic and you will become mentally weak. Make it your mission to always remain strong — the real man in control of any situation. It won't happen by reacting to every rude guy on the corner, every mean kid in school and every nut who calls you a stupid name. Don't give them your power. You need it for greater things.

Keep your power for your own purposes by pretending that you are holding a flashlight, which draws energy from the battery and projects it in the form of light toward an area you want to illuminate. When struggling with heavy emotions, think of your anger as a river of hot light. Act as if you are shining that light toward a way out of the woods (your problems) and not deeper into them.

In other words, you don't have to direct that beam toward the person who cut you off in traffic. You don't have to aim it at the smart-mouth kid next to you in the cafeteria. You can shift it to the pretty girl in front of you — or point it inward to think about all the trouble you'll find yourself in if you allow the darkness of blind rage to flood your soul. Feelings like that can storm through your body like a blast of thunder. What's more, they can push you to do things that will mess up your life, and it's never worth it.

It's not always easy, but you absolutely *must* keep a good grip on that imaginary flashlight. If you're having a hard time focusing on a pleasant way out of the woods, try humming your favorite tune, if you can't think of one, then what about the song "Happy" by Pharrell Williams? No one gets tired of hearing that feel-good song. When someone's trying to "bring you down," remember Pharrell's upbeat words:

> *Here come bad news, talking this and that, yeah,*
> *Well, give me all you got, and don't hold back, yeah,*
> *Well, I should probably warn you I'll be just fine, yeah,*
> *No offense to you, don't waste your time.*

Pharrell goes on to say that "can't nothing bring me down." He says he's happy and his "level's too high." How about you? Do you exist at such a low level that the least little thing can make you snap? Are you ready to blow up if someone looks at you too hard or wrong? Then it's time to get happy — search for ways to find and maintain those good feelings.

These suggestions might sound like gimmicks, but I know for a fact that they work. Don't think your generation is the first to ever get angry or picked on. We've all endured our share of jerks. When I was around nine years old, I developed a stuttering problem which, of course, made me a prime target for bullies. Day after day they taunted, called me names and threw rocks. I grew so tired of being their victim, I made up my mind to seek revenge. Fortunately, my mother and I talked about it first and she forbade me to strike back. She told me that she understood I was fed up and the bullies were wrong. But, she had no intention of allowing me to resort to aggression against anyone. Although my mother was firm, she was also tender and loving. Her exact words were: "Love your enemy."

I was too young to fully understand the concept, but since it came from my mother, I had to go along. I soon began to realize that the bullies had their own problems that had nothing to do with me. Something else had caused their behavior, something missing or broken within themselves and their lives. I developed a new perception of kids who pick on others. Every time one angered me, I knew how to calm down.

Years later, when a kid *lied* to my middle-school football coach that I was a bully and had been giving him a hard time, I was so hurt I really did feel like beating him up, especially when I saw that the coach actually believed his terrible story. But, I knew that would only make things worse. So, I took all that energy onto the football field, where I played like a demon standout that day, ripping and running through practice. By the end of the evening, I had tired myself out and wasn't nearly so upset. Once you quiet your mind, the voice of reason returns. You may still be mad, but you'll be able to think more clearly and handle the situation with maturity in a way that's not going to just create more problems.

You always have a future to think about. You have graduation coming up, a senior prom to look forward to, and a job or college to consider. And if your circumstances are anything like mine when I was a teen, you also have a lot of people counting on you to pull through and make them proud.

No one instilled such expectations in poor R.J., who, as a result, might go through life believing that getting mad makes him "the man." He may never realize that true men know how to rise above the petty upsets of life. Tempers will flare on occasion and resentment will rise up within. Righteous men release it because they know it won't get them anywhere but in trouble. The only thing to be done with anger and fury is to transform them into something positive.

As with anything, controlling your temper takes practice. At first, it might seem hard, but it's really no more difficult or uncommon than any other life skill. Remember what it was like learning to ride a bike? You focused on a certain tree you wanted to reach, or told yourself you were going to make it all the way to a house near the end of the block. You held on tight and — *wham*, you fell. Then you tried again, then again and yet again. After a few days or maybe even weeks, you found yourself pedaling a little farther and moving along with a lot more confidence. It was all in your mind all the time.

When you're used to losing your temper, you keep losing your temper. You're not disciplining yourself to do things any other or better way. So the next time you get mad, pay attention to what's going on inside of you — the frustration, the fluttering heart, the shouts you hear pouring from your own mouth. Pick one of those reactions and start training your mind to tone it down. If you're prone to frequent outbursts, practice more positive and productive reactions:

• Take a long deep breath. As you exhale, slowly count to 10.

• Quickly ask yourself: Is this going to matter next week? Will it matter a month from now? Next year, will I even remember?

• Picture yourself on your favorite ride at an amusement park Concentrate on that image and feeling, and hold it as long as you can.

• Try to zero in on a pleasant emotion. This is a tough one, but it can be done. Right now would be a great time to think of something beforehand so you have it on file and ready to deploy the moment your mind starts spinning away from you. Think of the funniest thing you've ever seen or heard, then call it up with your next angry thought to help step it down.

• Pretend that the person who is making you angry is wearing a crazy outfit. Make it as funny or unstylish as necessary. Picture him with no teeth or a fuzzy tail. Imagine anything silly or crazy enough to reset your mind.

• If you can, try to hold onto something very cold like a can of soda, popsicle or handful of ice cubes. It has been proven that cold objects can ease tension in the body and reduce feelings of anger.

Being a man means you alone are responsible for what you feel, say and do. That means you have to develop personal strategies and outrageous techniques of your own to collect yourself after getting worked up. You will get mad sometimes. We all do. Just understand that good people don't let every little insult or problem turn them into an uncontrollable madman like the Incredible Hulk

So, someone talked about you? Let it go. They laughed at you? Picture them wearing goofy, outdated clothes and move on. Save your passion for something major. Stop and chill first. No matter how rattled you are, please understand that "going HAM," as Kanye West and his many admirers put it, may sell rap music, but is never the best solution in real life. It's more important to keep a cool head so you can think your way logically through the worst of situations. Don't perpetuate the destructive thug culture that makes a few men like Kanye rich enough, but the rest of us all the poorer. Try what's unfortunately become the unexpected — share a few jokes or light-hearted comments with your so-called enemy. Change the conversation and charter the course in a different direction.

Comedian Chris Rock once used humor to make people laugh so he could get out of fights and avoid trouble. Richard Pryor, a well-known comic from the '70s and '80s, turned to comedy to tone down his explosive "fits of anger." Other comedians like Steve Harvey, Cedric the Entertainer, Jim Carrey, Sinbad, Jimmy Fallon and Detroit's CP say jokes were an escape for them, too. Coco, a Detroit-area radio personality and comedienne, says that as a full-figured student, she became the class clown in high school to cope with all the kids who ridiculed her about her weight.

That's what it means to *think before you act.* Wait before doing something desperate. Sweep out your brain before you start plotting ways to get even or cause harm. If you have a bad history with someone in particular, inhale slowly then leave the situation immediately. Go do some jumping jacks, jog around the block or take a cool shower; turn up your music — preferably without HAM in it — to distract your thoughts and actions. Whatever you do, unclench those fists. Don't start swinging every time somebody says something that rubs you the wrong way.

Talk things over with a friend, cool teacher or uncle. You might also benefit from really lashing out with boxing gloves at the nearest gym. Hitting a punching bag is one of the best ways to release anger and frustration, and will get the rest of your body in good shape along with your mind.

Life is like a game of dodge ball. You're going to get hit and you're going to go down now and then. Don't get up looking for a reason to beat someone else down. Look for the lesson in the experience — like keeping your head on a swivel, anticipating and reacting faster next time. Then jump right back into the game. Tell yourself that you learned a thing or two. You're smarter now. Because of a certain bad experience, you're becoming as tough as a heavy-weight dodge ball pro, ready for just about anything. You'll lose your patience again, there's no doubt about it. But, don't let it have a negative impact on you or someone else.

If you follow the advice you've just read, the blow-ups will fade away, your rage will melt and you will develop the true maturity of self-control. Remember, no natural force is of much use to us unless it is confined and focused in the right direction. Think about that the next time you get a little hot under the collar. As motivational speaker and author Napoleon Hill once said: "Our mind is the only thing we can control. Either we control it or we relinquish control to other forces."

CHAPTER 5

BELIEVE IN YOURSELF

"Don't pretend to be what you're not, instead, pretend to be what you want to be; it is not presence, it is a journey to self-realization."
— Michael Bassey Johnson

I truly care about each of you. I care what happens to all young people. I wish I could tell every young man that everything he needs most in life will be given to him. But I don't, because I know it's not the case. Many are willing to help all they can. But in the final analysis, you alone are the *master of your fate and captain of your soul,* as the English poet William Ernest Henley put it in 1875.

A century later, Nelson Mandela repeated that famous phrase to himself every night during his 27 years in prison for taking a stand against racial apartheid in South Africa. Mandela's own "unconquerable soul" empowered him to endure harsh injustice — "My head is bloody, but unbowed," Mandela also wrote— until he was released from captivity in 1990. He then helped lead the final revolution against minority white rule and became president of a new democratic South Africa in 1994. What an inspirational example of believing in yourself. Be it money, a break in life, good grades or the girl of your dreams, those things aren't going to happen unless you follow one little sacred rule: *Believe in yourself.*

Those three words form one of the most powerful statements in the universe. When you believe in yourself, doors open. Your friends, classmates and even adults are more likely to listen to what you have to say because they believe in you as well.

This is one of the most basic principles of life. But, too many men, young and old, fail to achieve it. Oh sure, they speak loud and talk a lot of trash. Some even have what I call "fake swag" — they wear stylish clothes, hang around with the popular kids at school, tell lies and put people down. Most of their behavior is a weak attempt to attract attention and convince others they've got it going on. However, it's easy to see that they are nothing but imposters and posers.

Real confidence is like a sorcerer's spell. You don't have to yell or walk a certain way. You don't have to tease others or wear expensive fabric that makes you stand out. It's more like something that shines from within in the way you carry yourself and interact with others. It's a magnetic quality that attracts good things to you and helps you make good things happen.

Call it self-worth, self-esteem, or self-empowerment, it all adds up to liking the person who is always with you. Some of you will quickly respond to that, of course, you like yourself. Some might even think you're so confident, you could write this chapter yourself, but reading it would be a waste of time. I challenge you to venture into that secret place in your head where no one is speaking or listening but you. Now what are you really, really hearing there? What do you whisper quietly to yourself when you fail an exam or get benched from a basketball game? How do you explain it when a girl turns you down, when people laugh or talk about you? What do you think about when nothing is going your way?

At times like this, do doubt and negative ramblings sneak into your mind? Do you feel like giving up? Do you listen to the guys who are trying to convince you to join them on the corner and smoke a little weed? Or do you take control of your life and fight back?

If you are on the right road to genuine confidence, you never give up. You pat yourself on the back and fill your mind with any one of numerous positive messages:

- "I'm the man no matter what others say."
- "I got it going on and I know it."
- "I am a magnet for all things positive."
- "I deserve the best and I know the best is on the way."
- "I am powerful and brilliant. I am in control."

These statements are positive affirmations, like new batteries for the spirit. I tell all young men, including my own son and grandsons, that if they want to stay on top of their game, whatever it might be, they better come up with some powerful words to help them stay focused by building and maintaining self-confidence.

Having it once doesn't mean it can't fade. Life sometimes chips away at pride and self-respect. Anyone who wants to keep it has to work at it. So go ahead, praise yourself. Stand at a mirror if you need to and brag about yourself. Come up with some exciting descriptions about your special qualities. Write down all the compliments you deserve then repeat them over and over again quietly in your mind. Be your own cheerleader and biggest fan.

That's how you sow the seeds of high self-esteem and nurture feelings of power. They're just like the flowers and leafy plants your mom might have around the house. If you want bigger swag, more exciting goals and a larger than life presence, you have to water your mind with larger than life ideas every single day.

Back in my day, there was as a budding NFL Hall of Famer by the name of Joe Namath, also known as "Broadway Joe." Everyone loved him, especially the ladies. He was handsome, arrogant and a star quarterback for the New York Jets. He once told a talk-show host that every evening he would tell himself: "I get better looking every day. I can't wait until tomorrow."

You have to admit, that's better than putting yourself down. I'd rather hear about a young man pumping himself up any day than one who constantly tells himself that he can't do this or can't accomplish that. If you believe you can do it, you can. If you believe you can't, then of course you can't.

My grandson is at that precious yet vulnerable age when the mind is like a sponge absorbing everything he hears, good or bad. So, I tell him all the time that he can do whatever he wants to do. Then I encourage him to tell himself the same. It's important that he hears positive words rattling around in his own head, but also to repeat those words and make them a natural part of his consciousness. They will create excitement in his mind, body and soul. They will generate enthusiasm and build unbeatable confidence. If he holds on to them, he will begin to take them very seriously. Remember the R. Kelly song, "I Believe I Can Fly"? Well, that's what I want my grandson and all young men to believe. You believe it by telling yourself, then telling yourself again and again.

You must recognize that there is no one in the world exactly like you. There are others with similar abilities, personalities and facial features; they may even have the same name and mannerisms, likes and dislikes. Yet, no one adds up exactly like you. Everything that comes from you is truly yours because you alone were born with or chose it. You own everything about you — your body, including everything it does, your mind and all of its thoughts, and your eyes with all they see, believe and envision.

You own your anger, joy, frustration, love, disappointment and excitement, and the same goes for your mouth and all the words that come out of it — polite, sweet, rough, right or wrong. Your voice belongs to you, loud or soft, as do all your dreams, hopes and fears. You must know yourself well to be your own best friend. Block out negative comments from others that only reflect their own self-doubt. Honor and work on parts that don't measure up. Be honest, but love your whole self completely and unconditionally.

That's the tricky part. Loving yourself doesn't mean being loud, acting out to get attention or wearing designer clothes. It means honestly admiring and respecting all your personal qualities because you've deliberately chosen and cultivated them for carefully considered reasons. If there is something that needs to be changed, you care enough to recognize and change it. If there is something that others have criticized unjustly, drown out their negativity and honor yourself anyway.

You love yourself by seeing the good in yourself. Do you have a great smile? Do you make other people laugh? Maybe you can play ball. Maybe you're extra smart in math. What is it that makes you unique? Are you helpful? Are you considerate? Can you run pretty fast? Are you a good roller skater? Can you fix things? Do you know how to dance? There is something extra special going on inside you and it's up to you to embrace that quality every day. Here are a few steps to get you in the habit:

- Stand in the mirror and admire your favorite physical traits — nice skin, bright eyes, thick head of hair, muscular body. Say something positive to yourself. Say it out loud and with passion.

- Think about your personality and praise at least one non-physical trait. If you're shy, remind yourself that you're probably a deep thinker — the creative type who writes books, screenplays, poems and even rap songs. If you're outgoing, take pride that you're probably a lot of fun to be around. Think of all the careers — radio announcer, deejay, trial lawyer, salesman, teacher — that require the gift of gab.

- Reflect on something someone said to you that didn't feel so good. Now think of ways to turn it around. Honestly consider the truth of it before concluding that it was either unjustified or something you should, can and will improve upon. Think about all the reasons you can reach your goals. Think of the talents and knowledge you do have. Hold those thoughts in your mind throughout the day.

- Before you go to sleep each night, repeat the first two steps.

It is that simple. Believing in yourself is as basic as saying it. If you think and stay positive, you'll get positive results. Just about anyone who has ever achieved their dream will tell you they once had potentially crippling moments of self-doubt, but didn't give in to them. They held their ground by finding another belief and clinging to it. They claimed it. They practiced it. Then before long, they owned it.

Motivational speaker Anthony Robbins frequently says that anything any human being can do, you can do as well or better. I agree 100 percent. Given proper study and equal opportunity, you can do anything anybody else can do regardless of what others may have told you. No one nation, race or ethnic group has a monopoly on brains. God spread intelligence around in such a way that we have genius coming out of rural areas, suburbs, urban communities and inner-city neighborhoods otherwise known as 'hoods. It doesn't matter who you are or where you're from. It's all about patting yourself on the back, accepting the person you are and believing in the amazing man you are capable of becoming.

If you don't have or cultivate sufficient reasons to like yourself, it's going to be tough to navigate life's storms. It is crucial that you be committed so you can feel as deserving as anyone else. You must put yourself eye to eye with your peers — not looking down or up at anyone. See yourself as equal to the studies, the job and the career path of your choice.

One of the world's most interesting insects is the bumblebee. It has a roly-poly body and short, stubby wings. By the most obvious laws of physics, it should not be able to fly. But, the bumblebee has never taken a physics class so doesn't know about this so-called limitation. It not only flies, but zooms all over the place completely unaware that it is accomplishing an amazing physical feat.

Many of you *will* be told or made to feel at some point, "You can't do that, you're black, Hispanic, or poor." Unlike the bumblebee, you will be able to hear these negative comments, both spoken and implied. You might even start to agree with the naysayers after a while when you should just ignore them and keep zooming to greater heights. Be what you want to be. Become your own masterpiece and marvel of nature. Do the great things that you believe you can achieve.

The April 1988 issue of *Ebony Magazine* contained a true story that young men of today need to hear. It concerned Ron McNair, a young black male from Lake City, a small town in South Carolina. There wasn't much to do and very few opportunities in Lake City when he graduated as valedictorian of his segregated high school class in 1967. But because this young man wanted to go further, he left South Carolina to attend North Carolina A&T State University. When he told an administrator that he wanted to major in physics, he was asked if he studied the subject in high school.

"No, they didn't teach physics at the black school in Lake City," he replied.

"Well, Ron, we don't know whether you can do it or not," the administrator responded.

But McNair was a bumblebee who had already caused a stir at the age of 9, when he refused to leave Lake City's whites-only public library until being allowed to borrow books. No one ever persuaded him that black boys from Lake City couldn't read what they wanted or pursue any college degree of interest. He not only majored in physics, but graduated from A&T with honors.

Next, he had to decide what to do with his life. Someone suggested the prestigious Massachusetts Institute of Technology (MIT). Like a good bumblebee, he applied and was accepted. McNair did so well, in 1976 he became one of the first black scholars to receive a Ph.D. in physics from MIT. Yet, he didn't stop there.

His next stop was California, lured by the prospect of flying into space. At the time, this was a pretty audacious goal for anyone, especially someone of color. He wouldn't be the first, but in those days many still believed that blacks couldn't — or shouldn't — become anything of consequence, including space travelers. He paid them no mind either, became an astronaut and in 1984, served as a crewmember aboard the space shuttle *Challenger*. Two years later, he was among seven astronauts selected for his second Challenger mission to release a satellite to photograph Halley's Comet. Thirteen seconds after take-off the Challenger exploded, plummeting in pieces into the Atlantic Ocean.

No right-thinking humanist, including most certainly McNair himself, would suggest that his tragic end means he shouldn't have chased his dream of space travel. Dreams are like a divine appointment with destiny in all of our lives. If we don't pursue them, we get nowhere. It's up to us as men to dream as big as we can. This is what McNair did. His life may have been short, but it was filled with meaning and purpose. He followed and realized his passion, in the process receiving endless awards and a well-deserved place in history — not for how he died, but how he lived. He believed in himself enough to create the life he wanted.

It's a worthy example for everyone to live by. We make ourselves into what we want by reaching deep inside and moving forward in faith. All journeys into manhood are variously difficult and intimidating at times. You're not on the road by yourself. There's an old saying, "Everyone you meet is just as scared as you are."

Well, everyone that is, but the bumblebee.

CHAPTER **6**

HAVE A BACKUP PLAN

"Failing to plan is planning to fail."
— Alan Lakein

There is an old folktale about a dog whose experience can teach us a lot about life. The dog in the tale was carrying a bone across a rickety bridge that arched over a wide river. He was pretty protective of his bone. His jaws were clenched tightly around it and he repeatedly sniffed in the air and looked around him to make sure no one was trying to steal his prize.

The bridge swung and cracked noisily as the nervous dog hurried to the other side. However, when he got close to the end, he thought he noticed something in the river. He looked down and saw another dog also carrying a very large, appealing bone.

Of course, it was really his own reflection, but he didn't know that. He was convinced that he was staring at a rival with his teeth clamped on something desirable. The bone looked so delicious that the dog on the bridge decided to try and take it. He growled ferociously, hoping to scare the dog in the river into giving it up. But as his jaws opened, he lost his grip on his dinner. As he watched helplessly, it splashed and disappeared into the water.

There are several lessons to this story: It's good to want more out of life and to focus on big goals. But, it's not okay to prey on others at the much greater expense of your own honesty and integrity. Ambition is wonderful, but greed is negative and unproductive. Like jealousy and envy, it gets you worse than nowhere — and all for something that's just an illusion. Whatever you do, don't foolishly throw away what you already have in order to pursue something uncertain.

In other words, make sure you have a backup plan. This plan, which can be considered your safety net over the water, is also known as plan B. It's the situation, career, job or opportunity that you can depend on if something goes wrong with plan A.

Poker players call it their "ace in the hole," meaning the one card they can count on to win the game, if necessary. Maybe you want to be a hip-hop artist, but you're also good with numbers. So, the surest bet is to study accounting or finance — gain the knowledge and college degree that will always be your "ace in the hole" and afford you the opportunity to keep trying your hand with other cards.

You may be the rarest of exceptions who never needs a side hustle. Or you could be a mere mortal who most certainly will. Regardless, when you set high goals for yourself, you generally don't achieve them overnight. That's why a fallback plan is so important. It gives you legitimate options, support and a secure income. It provides the good times needed to get through the tough ones.

I was reminded of this when I read about a young man who absurdly turned down a fully paid, four-year college scholarship because he wanted to pursue a rap career. I'm not sure how his parents reacted, but I was shocked. A college scholarship is an incredible opportunity, particularly when it covers all expenses. Obviously, this young man was a very bright student who made a not-so bright decision about his future.

His bad choice may have been partly inspired by the example of another rapper, Big Sean from Detroit. He also turned down a full scholarship to Michigan State University before releasing his aptly named debut album, *Finally Famous*, five years later in 2011 — at around the same time he could also have graduated with a college degree. But, the reality remains that Sean Henderson's relatively rapid success was an exception and not the norm. It could always happen again to someone else, but ask yourself: If instant fame, success and wealth are so easy, why isn't everyone doing it?

Like professional sports, spectacular entertainment careers are for those with superhuman talent, extraordinary effort and phenomenal luck. When the very few do make it that far, there's still no guarantee that their flash will last longer than a firefly on a hot summer night.

Don't think I'm trying to discourage you from anything. To the contrary, I'm actually rooting for you. I'm on your side. I want you to dream big. I want you to reach for the moon. At the same time, I want you to use common sense that seems lacking among too many starry-eyed young people today.

According to scholar and African studies expert Dr. Henry Louis Gates, many black students place more emphasis on singing or sports careers than they do on getting a college education. The sad truth is that an overwhelming majority never get close to their big break. In an essay for *Sports Illustrated* magazine, Dr. Gates notes there are only 1,200 black professional athletes in all of the United States. To put that in perspective, 98 out of 100 high school athletes never even get to play collegiate sports, and only 1 out of 16,000 makes it to the pros.

If you are part of the minority with the exceptional talent required to join that elite 1,200, then by all means push and work at it as hard as you can. However, once you read the rest of what Dr. Gates has to say, you will understand why I want all young men to focus on more than just playing ball or rapping.

He states that an "African American youngster has about as much chance of becoming a professional athlete as he or she does of winning a million dollars in the lottery." On the other hand, a college degree virtually guarantees you'll make a million dollars or more over your lifetime. That's why there are about 36 times more black lawyers, black dentists and black doctors than black athletes.

This would be a good time to ask yourself what you might do with an extra million dollars — not as a daydreamer standing in line for a lottery ticket, but as someone with a sure thing in your future if you just start reaching for it now. Does this give you something to think about? It should. It means you are living in an era that offers you an entire buffet of choices. Don't limit yourself. Don't drop a sure thing for something that could be an illusion. And whatever you do, don't follow the example of anyone who throws away an opportunity to go to college — especially for free — in return for the reflection of a shiny object in the water.

There's nothing wrong with big dreams and calculated career risks. But, there's a huge difference between smart risks and poor decisions. If there's little to no likelihood of success on one hand but every reason to expect it on the other, doesn't it make more sense to at least do them both?

Nothing stops the would-be rapper from attending school during the day and doing his other thing on the weekends. He can spend a few hours studying and a few more writing music. If he's good enough, he should be able to pick up gigs even while getting an education. Not everyone knows this but the actor Hill Harper, whose TV roles include *CSI: New York* and *Covert Affairs*, is also an attorney. In fact, he attended Harvard University's Law School with President Barack Obama. He uses his intellect to write best-selling books and his talent to shine on TV and in movies like For *Colored Girls* and *Lackawanna Blues*.

Likewise for veteran rapper Young MC. Although he was really interested in a hip-hop career, he was smart enough to pursue a degree in economics from Columbia University. While he was at the university, he met two guys who just happened to have their own recording company. I guess you know what happened after that. Young MC was discovered. He hit it big right off as the songwriter for Tone Loc's "Wild Thing." Then he went on to release his biggest smash, "Bust a Move," a Grammy-winning tune from 1989 that's still being played on the radio, used in movie soundtracks and nearing 10 million views on YouTube.

Despite "Bust a Move" and several follow-up albums over the next 25 years, Young MC never got another big break in the entertainment industry. Fortunately, because of his college degree, he had other options, and now spends his time writing screenplays and doing voiceover work for commercials. Even if you go on to do something entirely unrelated to a specific college major, the universal knowledge of higher education is never a waste of time or money. Some aspect of the experience will serve you well in just about any situation you can imagine for yourself.

Hip-hop artists J. Cole and even 2 Chainz are also well-rounded college grads. They, too, are examples of what happens when we tap into all of our talents and strengths. They represent what it means to hold on tight and go after multiple goals while keeping your "eyes on the prize" awaiting those who exercise their full range of brains, talent and hustle.

Here's something more about that prize: As you make your way through middle school, high school or even college, you'll need a guide to point you in the right direction. Whether you realize it or not, older people can teach you all you need to know about juggling responsibilities and staying on the right track. That is what we are here for.

During the Civil Rights Movement of the 1950s and 60s, your grandfathers and great-grandfathers dealt with injustice and other hardships by staying focused on their goals. The term "eyes on the prize" was in fact born out of a movement that forced black men and women to endure extreme difficulties while working toward their dreams. I know because I was part of that important era. I worked hard and took my share of low-paying part-time jobs, but always kept my eyes glued to a greater cause and purpose.

Later, the term "multi-tasking" became popular during the computer age to describe people who can juggle numerous assignments at the same time. It's actually a much older concept that comes as naturally to the young men of today as it always has to busy people in the past. You are a gifted generation of quick learners and deep thinkers with a unique skill for handling all things technological. You can play a video game, download music, read and send text messages, use your cell phone to record a video and post it on Instagram all within the same five minutes. You're filled with curiosity, unprecedented opportunity, and a tremendous amount of mental and physical energy.

Use that energy wisely. Invest some of it into traditional education and some on your passion for painting, singing, dancing or shooting hoops. As they used to say long before computers, "Don't put all your eggs in one basket." Chart a future that will create multiple streams of income. Think big, but be practical. Don't get caught up in anything that involves shady deals, quick money or the promise of overnight success. Nothing worth having is ever that easy, but losing it all like the poor dog on the bridge is a very real possibility for those who don't think and plan ahead.

7

IS IT A PROBLEM
OR A PUSH?

If you risk nothing, then you risk everything.
— Geena Davis

It is a cool, windy morning and a mother eagle is leading her babies to the edge of a steep cliff. As they approach the upward air currents, the little ones pause. They realize the cliff is pretty dangerous and they're afraid of plunging to the ground far below.

The mother gently nudges, but the babes refuse to move. So she gives them a firm push. That push is her supreme act of faith and love. Their uncertain wings flutter at first. Then they flap once or twice before being overtaken by destiny. With one swoosh, the wind catches their wings and the little eagles soar.

You, too, are standing near the edge, preparing to take your first flight into adulthood. Sometimes, like eagles, young men also need to be pushed. And that is exactly what life does. But when it happens, you might not recognize it as a nudge that is moving you closer to greatness. Instead, you'll probably call it something else — a problem.

When life is trying to move us forward, we often feel that pressure under our wings in the form of an illness, a breakdown in family life, chaos at school or some other personal crisis. We may even get so overwhelmed that we want to withdraw from the world. That's not the answer. Hardship nudges us in a different, often better direction. Tough times are sometimes the jolt we need just to wake up and try something new.

The girl or team that turns you down might be doing you a favor if their rejection inspires you to work twice as hard to pump yourself up. Being tricked makes you more likely to spot a liar next time. Dealing with turmoil at home builds inner strength and determination. In his absence or poverty, a father's example can teach you to do much better when it's your turn.

Even if you have experienced tragedy, you're more mature because of it. You can't have a devastating experience and not grow up. Whether it is the loss of a loved one or some other misfortune, trauma helps young people understand cause and effect — and that all actions have consequences.

Difficulties are often just blessings and opportunity in clever disguise. They are the mountains you trudge to greater heights. They are only negative if you don't turn them into positives. But that decision is up to you alone. You are the one who must allow the treacherous rocks on your path to become stepping stones to a better future.

When I was young, I had an aunt who was very mean to me. Her son (my cousin) had nice toys and clothes, which I didn't. She treated me differently and made me feel somehow inferior to her son. Rather than accepting or believing that, I worked harder in school to prove her wrong.

I often think of the story about a little boy and girl who were climbing up a long, bumpy trail toward the top of a hill. The girl whined about the path's unevenness, but her older brother said, "Little sister, don't complain about the bumps. It is the bumps that we climb on to get us to the top." And so it is true in our lives. We grow by confronting resistance, adversities and problems. In finding solutions, we discover hidden abilities. We adapt to become more efficient and effective.

There are abundant examples of this throughout nature. Take the cobra, for instance. Like most snakes, the cobra has to shed its skin every three months. But, it also needs help getting started. It must slither against some sharp or jagged object until feeling a sting. This pain is essential because it indicates the object has caught a piece of skin. As the snake pulls away, the snagged skin tears so the rest of it begins to peel and shed.

The snake would not enjoy a smooth new underbelly without first undergoing this bit of struggle. Disappointments can cut or hurt us too, but if properly handled they become a wonderful source of strength and rejuvenation.

Remember the ancient advice: "If someone throws a dagger or knife at you and you catch it by the blade, it will cut you. If you catch it by the handle, you use it for your own defense." What happens to us matters less than what happens in us. It's not what goes wrong that counts, but our response to it.

Your hard times might be such a burden that you'd do anything to make them go away. You're convinced that this hardship has visited your life to either destroy you or make you a miserable failure forever. Change that outlook now. Don't use challenges as an excuse for anger and depression. Everything that hurts you also makes you stronger.

When I was in the fourth grade, I had a teacher who placed everyone in special groups according to how well they were doing in a specific subject. At the time, I wasn't a good speller and felt very embarrassed to be in the green spelling group. That was a terrible way to teach, but it motivated me to get out of the green group that had become the butt of jokes at school. With 20 words to learn, I went over them again and again until I mastered every single letter of each. I began to excel at spelling, found joy in the midst of the challenge, and learned a greater love for words and reading that has stayed with me ever since.

If you look for the good, you will always find it. Every time you fall, don't get up ready to start swinging, whining, complaining or blaming. Get up and fight to be better. When you have a bad experience, turn it around by looking for what you can get out of it. Think of it as a push. See yourself on a cliff with the eagles. Accept your challenge as a shove that's encouraging you to reach higher — forcing you to activate your potential. Recognize it as an opportunity in the making.

If people are putting you down, do you lose faith in yourself or make up your mind to prove them wrong? Do you allow hatred and bitterness to get trapped inside of you or release it by trying to learn a lesson from your setbacks and mistakes? Everything we become is because of what we have overcome. That might be a cliché, but it contains powerful truth. Consider these examples:

• Oprah Winfrey was working as a TV news reporter in Baltimore when she was suddenly pulled off the air by a producer who told her she would never make it in that capacity. Oprah was devastated. To cheer up, she accepted a lowly job with daytime TV. The show skyrocketed and so did her career.

• When Art Briles was 20 years old, his parents died in a car accident. Grief stricken, Briles channeled all the pain into his sports career. He is now a well-known college football coach who specializes in transforming failing football teams into champions.

• As a toddler, future rap sensation LL Cool J watched helplessly as his dad shot his mom. She later remarried and he was abused by his stepdad. But LL, who was born with a bad arm, "pushed" himself to success. He strengthened his arm and the rest of his body by working out constantly. He built his mind and career by pouring all of his energy into his music.

• Actor James Earl Jones stuttered so badly as a child that he needed speech therapy. He worked hard to conquer his limitation, became a master speaker and distinguished actor His booming voice is now the signature sound of Darth Vader in the *Star Wars* series and the unmistakable bass who announces daily, "This is CNN."

• Jerry Seinfeld's TV show *Seinfeld* was so popular its primary actors earned a million dollars per episode. But, his career didn't exactly start with a bang. He did standup comedy in tiny night clubs before eventually landing a small role on a sitcom called *Benson*. But the producers didn't like him or his character. One morning, he showed up for work only to find that his role was cancelled and he had been fired. Embarrassed and afraid of going broke, he headed back to weekend standup. His humility paid off when a talent scout caught Seinfeld's act and offered him his own sitcom, which became the most successful TV show of all time.

• Years ago Patrick Rhoden, who lived in a small village in Jamaica, was shot by a stranger and paralyzed from the waist down. Although he made the best of it, his disability prevented him from earning enough money to support his family. He had to do odd jobs and rely on a motorized wheelchair to get around. To make matters worse, the wheelchair broke down and none of the repair shops in Jamaica had parts to fix it. Despondent, Rhoden almost lost faith before turning to friends and family for financial help. In several months, they scraped together enough money to fly him to the U.S., where he didn't just purchase parts but enrolled in a class that taught him how to repair wheelchairs. When he returned home, he began fixing them all over Jamaica. He is now happier and wealthier than before the shooting.

These are just a few stories of well-known people whose lives improved after serious setbacks. The list is endless — from author, J.K. Rowling, who was behind in her rent when a New York publishing house bought her first "Harry Potter" book, to Rubin "Hurricane" Carter, the middle-weight prize fighter who was unjustly imprisoned for 19 years. Carter used his time behind bars to read, write, meditate and become a symbol of triumph within the human spirit.

There are also countless examples of less-famous people who allowed despair to bring out the best in them. You may have even encountered a few yourself who make you wonder how they manage to keep going with such positive attitudes. Rather than sink into hopeless depression, they find ways to turn their bad times into profit, social justice and personal triumph. How about you? As you navigate through the turbulence of life, are you going to give up whenever you encounter difficulty? Are you going to see it as a problem or understand that it's just another "push" in a different direction?

Former TV talk-show host Montel Williams has a unique way of grappling with life's hard knocks. He used to travel across the country explaining his approach at schools and community centers packed with teens. His message was simple and direct: He told young people to think of themselves as bigger than any obstacle. Look around them, he said. Look above them and beyond. Then stand tall as a soldier, hold your shoulders back and shout, *Hey mountain, get out of my way!*

CHAPTER

"Remember: the time you feel lonely is the time you most need to be by yourself. Life's cruelest irony."

— Douglas Coupland

So there you are, at home on a Saturday night, reading a book or strategizing about a new project, a new goal or some gadget you hope to invent. In the back of your mind, you may have a picture of a more ideal way to spend your evening.

Perhaps, you should stop by a friend's house, go to a party or, at the very least, call a girl and ask her to a movie. But, you stop yourself. You keep reading. You keep studying. You continue to brainstorm for new ideas.

What's wrong with you?

The answer is simple: You are taking a temporary walk through the land of solitude. In the process, you are learning more about yourself, you are preparing yourself for the future and you are discovering the power of thought.

Thought is a powerful weapon and when you make a deliberate attempt to fill your mind with positive thoughts about where you want to go and the path you want to take, you might find yourself on a lonely journey.

You reach out to talk to others and they don't understand. Your friends like it when you call to chat about the game, but not many of them want to hear about the deeper ideas that might be flowing through your mind. So, you lock them inside and keep them to yourself. You spend hours pouring your ideas onto paper. You spend weekend evenings quietly dreaming.

It may seem like a trap that's hard to escape, but time alone leads to great success. When you are striving and achieving, you have to step off the traditional path sometimes and find your own little corner. Everyone is not going to understand you during these moments — and that's okay.

It can be lonely at the top.

From your perspective, that might sound like a strange statement. At this point in your life, the top could be as far away as Mount Everest. The top might seem like a fictitious planet inhabited by Jedi Knights from *Star Wars*.

But no, it is not. The top is the destination of those who spend time alone thinking, planning and cherishing ideas that others might not feel like discussing. It's not that your friends aren't interested in you anymore. It's just that your ideas are dreamy-eyed and your concerns might include more than buying pizzas and the latest pair of Air Jordans.

It's sort of like the difference between being a Boy Scout and a Boy Scout leader. The scout gets to have fun all the time, but the leader has to spend time in his own little private space, figuring out ways to direct the pack. The good news is that the leader — the one who spends time deep in thought — is smart, interesting and successful. The not-so-good news is that the leader will sometimes feel lonely.

Trust me, this lonely feeling will not last forever. So when you feel it, my suggestion is that you embrace it. Loneliness gives you the space to reflect and examine why you are here and what you were meant to do. It is not a bad thing. The problem arises when we see our loneliness as a disability. We use it as an excuse for self-doubt and self-pity. This is a dangerous attitude that does us more harm than the loneliness itself.

In the book, *White Oleander*, by Janet Fitch, occasional loneliness is called an important part of being human. She describes it this way:

"Loneliness is the human condition. Cultivate it. The way it tunnels into you, allows your soul room to grow. Never expect to outgrow loneliness. Never hope to find people who will understand you, someone to fill that space. An intelligent, sensitive person is the exception, the very great exception. If you expect to find people who will understand you, you will grow murderous with disappointment. The best you'll ever do is to understand yourself, know what it is that you want, and not let the cattle stand in your way."

In this passage, the cattle Janet Fitch refers to are the everyday people leading everyday lives. When you are lonely, you are standing apart from them. The lessons you learn in the process will one day help guide the herd. This is something I had to figure out at a young age. I was blessed to have caring and loving parents who inspired me and served as my source of strength. They taught me what I needed to know to navigate through my emotions and the various experiences I encountered in life.

Without this type of guidance, it might be a little tougher to figure out what to do when you run into roadblocks. If you're feeling alone, this can be even more challenging. But, believe it or not, there's a hidden blessing in all situations. For instance, if you have to face hard times all by yourself, you will develop more mental muscle than most teens.

You will be stronger, wiser and more determined than your peers. You will also stumble upon something most don't figure out until they get older – you'll find out that the only person you need to be there for you is the person who is there all the time. That person is you. Be there for yourself. Be your own best friend. Don't let yourself down. Look within and find the golden truth buried in your own soul.

If you can do that, you have not only mastered the challenges of loneliness, you have also found a treasure that will stay with you forever. Use this inner strength to propel you through life. If you need to, find added support by seeking out resources, programs and youth guidance centers in your community. Also, remind yourself that alone time will not last forever. While you're in the midst of it, my advice is that you try to enjoy it. Allow it to be the magic carpet that will eventually give you what you need to soar over the storms of life.

Keep in mind that everyone is lonely in various ways and in varying degrees. It's just a matter of learning to cope with it. Remember that torch I spoke about in chapter four? When you use it to find your way out of the woods, the light will fall on faces that are meant to help you. In fact, as you read these words, you should realize that I'm someone who is trying to serve as that torch. With this book, I'm trying to be here for you as well.

And I'm using my experiences as an example. Over the years, my life has taught me that there are several benefits to being alone. Here are a few of them:

When left by ourselves to think and to analyze our own life events, our minds are almost on auto-pilot. Eventually, from a long chain of thoughts, decisions emerge. Solitude does that. It is my belief that decisions made during these periods are almost always correct. We tend to go with the flow of our thoughts and the pros and cons of every situation come clearly to our minds. Since there is no outside disturbance, we almost know that we can trust our gut feelings. No matter how much you explain a situation to anyone else in your life (a parent or a friend) only you know exactly how it feels. When we spend time with ourselves and contemplate, our minds guide us to make decisions that are in our own best interest.

When we are constantly interacting with others almost all of our waking time, our mind is forced to divert its energy toward the other person's thoughts and opinions. Their ideas influence us and steal our ability to look at things from our own perspective. When we allow ourselves to be alone and examine and understand our thoughts, situations or people that we could not comprehend earlier now become clearer. We see the forest, but we also see the trees. In other words, along with the smaller details, we learn to see the bigger picture.

To this day, I have made it a habit of spending time with myself. It benefits me to engage in a conversation with myself — perhaps because I cannot lie to myself or because no one understands me as much as I understand myself. I may not be able to share my concerns with anyone else completely on any topic, but I can relate it to myself. These conversations with myself lead me to make sensible and well-thought out decisions and, eventually, make me a stronger person. Solitude forces me to spend time with myself and talk to myself. It is in these moments that my fears disappear and I become a stronger person.

We all have experiences and moments in our lives that are unfortunate, even traumatic. We always hear the wise people tell us that when we emerge from these troubles, we will be stronger. I think this is true and this is why — when we revisit life's most troubling moments, we go through several phases mentally, including anger and rejection. However, when we continue to think about these experiences, especially when we are alone, we have a natural tendency to make peace with the past and reconcile. This reconciliation provides closure, which is vital for all of us to be able to move forward.

When we are emotional, we tend to think in extremes. When we sit alone and calmly analyze any situation, it allows us to be more rational. Things will not only disappear, but will also become more manageable. We tend to discover ways and strategies to deal with the challenges. We discover that we do have control over some of the things that happen to us. With this rationality, comes positivity. Positive thought is an amazing tool that helps even the most desperate to move forward. You gain confidence and begin to trust your ability to deal with tough times. Nothing will seem like the end of the world. It never is.

Sometimes, the best advice that we receive comes from within ourselves. If we are honest with ourselves and listen to our own hearts and minds, we recognize that they never lie to us. Whether we choose to listen to this advice is another matter. After all, humans are prone to denial and indiscretion. However, when we spend time quietly thinking our problems through, our minds and hearts tell us the right path of action. Even though it might be a difficult path, try following it anyway. Just know that even on dreary days, the sun is still shining behind the clouds.

Perhaps the greatest benefit of being with yourself is seeing a plan for your own future emerge from your thoughts. Somehow, we all tend to know what is good for us. A plan is just a series of small steps we need to take to make our lives better. The consistent courage to take small step after small step comes from within. It comes as a direct result of being with ourselves, thinking about our own good, listening to our inner voice and doing what our thoughts direct us to do. These small steps make a larger plan and I guarantee you that they are the only way to build a successful life.

So, if you believe you are alone, do not be afraid! Good things come out of solitude. And, even though it may not appear that way to you, everyone is alone in some way. It could be they are alone in their unique skills and talents. Maybe, no one gets their jokes and they are alone with their own odd sense of humor. Possibly, they feel loneliness within their daydreams, unusual habits or personal beliefs.

No matter what it is, everyone has a space that is their own private world. This is a power we all possess. When we control it, it will lead to thoughts, actions and, eventually, our own destiny.

WALK WITH COURAGE

"Courage is not the absence of fear, but rather the judgment that something else is more important than fear."
— Ambrose Redmoon

When I was in elementary school, I wanted to disappear.

I know it sounds odd, but that's how much sadness I felt back then. Like everyone else my age, I needed to fit in. I needed to be accepted. I needed to be one of the guys. But, the goal seemed impossible and, as a result, I felt the desire to vanish.

No doubt, someone — possibly someone reading this page right now — knows exactly what I'm talking about. I'm not sure what word you kids use to describe it, but in my day, it was the called the "in crowd." They were the hipsters, the popular ones, the young men everyone thought of as cool.

But, when it came to being cool, I had a special challenge — I stuttered uncontrollably. I mentioned this in an earlier chapter when I talked about the importance of controlling anger. In my situation, stuttering was a gift because it actually forced me to find ways to rise above the resentment and aggression I felt towards all the people who were teasing me. I discovered that if I focused my anger in another direction, the anger would go through a process I learned about in one of my science classes: It would evaporate.

Unfortunately for me, the anger was the only thing that evaporated. I still remained the butt of jokes and the subject of intense ridicule. I was called names. Rocks were thrown at me and dirt was kicked in my face.

Although I was successful at releasing my desire for revenge and channeling it into good study habits, that only solved one of my problems. It showed me how to become the master of my emotions, but it didn't stop the avalanche of bullies. And, it didn't help me to speak up when the teacher called on me in class. Nor did it assist me in my efforts to improve my boring reputation and low self-image.

I was painfully embarrassed. My stutter was so bad that I could hardly get a word out. I never made phone calls to friends and if someone called me, I didn't answer. I refused to give speeches in my English classes and I couldn't bring myself to ever approach a girl. That was out of the question. I felt there was no use in trying because, after all, my problem made me different from other kids.

Then, one day, I finally had enough. I was tired of feeling sorry for myself. So, instead of choosing to feel inferior, I simply made another choice. I chose courage.

It wasn't easy at first. But, I convinced myself to do it anyway. There is a book called *Feel the Fear and Do It Anyway* by Susan Jeffers. This author believes that our fears are our greatest teachers. Feeling afraid means that we're facing something we are supposed to conquer. According to Jeffers, when we conquer this fear, we change our lives.

There's another expression, "Do What Scares You!" This statement suggests that the challenges we want to avoid the most should be viewed as assignments. It is our duty to overcome them. Sound scary? Good. Think about something that sends chills up your spine. Now, what are you going to do about it? I suggest that you make a promise to yourself to deal with your challenge in a manner that is healthy and positive.

It doesn't have to be an enormous obstacle. It could be an ordinary, everyday worry like tasting a strange new food that's good for you or saving money that you would rather run out and spend on concert tickets and clothes. It could be a common fear like giving a speech or a secret wish you could play a sport that you're too afraid to try. Maybe you want to ice skate or try inline skates, while your friends prefer basketball. Are you afraid of what they might think of you?

Possibly, you'd like to talk to a school counselor about a problem at home, but fear is keeping you from walking into his or her office. Maybe you secretly would like to go to church, but you're worried that your boys might laugh at you. You're interested in Junior Achievement, but you're actually concerned that you might be called a nerd. Do you want to add a few big words to your vocabulary, but can't stand the idea that others might label you a snob?

It takes courage to believe in one's goals and to pursue them, despite the scorn of others. That's what Susan Jeffers means when she says, "Feel the Fear and Do It Anyway." That's the point of the slogan, "Do What Scares You!"

Although these particular books and mottos didn't exist when I was growing up, I came to that conclusion on my own. I saw my stuttering as a barbwire fence that I absolutely had to climb over. I knew I would get a few nicks, cuts and sores as I tried to get past this ugly roadblock. However, I told myself that I could either stay where I was — withdrawn and miserable, or I could force myself to do the very things that scared the daylight out of me.

So, I chose to stand up to my fears. That's when something wonderful happened inside of my spirit. I was filled with joy and, to my surprise, I began to feel unbeatable. For the first time in my life, I was holding my shoulders back and walking with my head up. I was opening my mouth and not worrying about how my words spilled out or how silly someone else thought I sounded.

I also discovered that it is not what is happening in our lives that matters. What matters is how we feel about what is happening. I realized, then and there, that life is not simply a series of incidents. No! Life is a series of choices. In fact, everything we do or don't do is the result of a choice. We can choose to take a back seat or we can choose to stand up for what we truly believe. We can choose to feel like a failure or we can pretend as if the word failure does not exist.

We can choose to fear rejection or we can choose to summon up the courage to face whatever it is that's holding us back. The day I chose courage, I knew I would be ignored by a whole lot of kids at school. I knew other kids would laugh when I stood up in class and stuttered through readings of my essays or passages in a workbook. I knew no one would be patient if I picked up the phone and called and I knew that it wouldn't be easy to walk up to a crowd and try to jump in to the conversation.

But, I did it anyway. And, you know what? It wasn't as bad as I thought it would be. Yes, others stared at me and, yes, there were snickers. A few kids even poked fun of me and imitated the way I talked. However, my mind was made up and I wasn't backing down.

Courage is like that. Once you adopt it, you feel powerful. Try it. Join the chess club. Write poetry, if you feel like it. Get an afterschool job as a janitor or a job walking the neighbor's dog.

Don't avoid doing something different just because it might feel awkward or attract criticism from your friends. Darrell Dawsey, a well-known journalist from Detroit, once shared a story about his tendency to pack books into his bedroom when he was still a teen. He loved literature, in spite of the fact that he lived in a rough neighborhood and didn't know many people who enjoyed reading. Some evenings, he hung out with his boys on the streets. But every night, he dabbled in his quiet hobby. As a result of his passion, he eventually went to college, became a writer for a number of major publications and the author of several books of his own.

But, it was a long and sometimes difficult journey. In his book, *Living to Tell About It, Young Black Men in America Speak*, Darrell Dawsey explains that he was constantly teased and called names by peers who visited him and were shocked by the library in his room. In one instance, he actually got into a fist fight with a buddy who taunted him and refused to back off.

I'm not encouraging you to take swings at people who taunt you, but I do see Dawsey's story as an amazing example of a young man who wasn't afraid to do what he really loved — even when his "love" didn't reflect the interests of those around him.

That is courage at its best.

When I found that level of courage, it no longer mattered to me that giggles were streaming from the back of the classroom or that it took me much longer to read than anyone else. It didn't matter that I couldn't talk the talk the way the other guys did while they hung out at the bus stop after school. All that mattered is that I had the nerve to chat with them. All that mattered is that I was doing my best.

From that day forward, I felt good enough about myself to overcome anything that stood in between me and my goals. Of course, it helped that my parents were on my side, encouraging me every step of the way. If you don't have the support of parents, then do what I suggested early on in the book: Talk to a mentor, a teacher, a relative or an older friend. Seek out the individual who will tell you what I'm telling you now.

CHOOSE COURAGE!

Do what it takes to leap over that hurdle, tackle that shortcoming and move forward. When you take the first step, you will suddenly feel a blast of new-found confidence and energy. That first step tells you that you are walking your walk. That step suggests that you are not afraid to be who you really are. Call it faith or call it enthusiasm, but that step will cause doors to swing open.

For me, the door that finally opened was my own willingness to challenge myself. I began to ask myself hard questions: Was I going to wallow in self-pity when I couldn't say a certain letter or word? Was I going to let myself be defined by my stutter or by other qualities such as my love for reading, my athletic skills and my likeable personality? Was I going to stay where I was or seek out the assistance and training that would allow me to improve? Was I going to believe I was stuck or develop the courage to master my speech impediment and learn to speak clearly and with power?

Courage is your friend. It is the absolute right choice to make. As Muhammad Ali once put it: "He who is not courageous enough to take risks will accomplish nothing in life."

NEVER TOO YOUNG TO LEAD

"The quality of a leader is reflected in the standards they set for themselves."
— Ray Kroc

Prior to his 2013 junior season, a stunning young Detroit high school superstar made a name and future for himself by leading his team to two division-one state championships as a freshman and sophomore quarterback. Brash, bright and good-looking, the young man (we will call him Tarik) won hearts all over the country and was already recruited to play for a top university. Then, he lost his cool — not once but twice — and it all went wrong in a hurry.

Tarik's high school got routed in its bid for a third consecutive championship by cross-town rival Mid-City Catholic Central, the same school it beat in both previous finals. In the handshake line after the 28-0 upset, he punched an opposing player and had to be restrained by his own teammates and coaches.

For that, he received a one-game suspension to be served in his senior year. It should have been a clear warning to re-examine his life so the incident could blow over and eventually be forgotten. But a few weeks later, when a school security guard asked him to remove his hoodie in compliance with the school's dress code, the 6-foot-4 athlete lost it again. He flew into a rage, grabbed the guard and body slammed him to the ground. Someone captured the incident on a cell phone and the video went viral.

Both are lucky the officer wasn't seriously hurt just for trying to keep the peace at school. It's a vital job any young leader of men should wholeheartedly admire and respect on or off the field. However, the 17 year old, described as one of the hardest working and smartest kids at the school, was sentenced to 60 days in jail for aggravated assault, a less-serious misdemeanor compared to the original felony charge of assault with intent to do great bodily harm. His athletic scholarship to Michigan State University has since vanished.

As of this writing, it remains to be seen if he can somehow redeem himself in his upcoming senior year so another college can give him a chance, or whether he goes down swinging at strike three instead. I'm still among those sincerely pulling for him to turn it around. Otherwise, his misplaced anger only serves as a vivid example of what happens when someone has no idea how to control their rage or cope with power and success. It's also a tragic reminder of how so many young men have much to learn about true leadership.

Leadership is fighting for what you believe in, not getting into scuffles to prove you're "bad." Leaders know when to fight, when to listen and when to be respectful. It would have taken more inner strength than violent, physical strength for the high-profile athlete to exercise self-control in both incidents. That's what a leader does — teaches by example. In that respect, we're all leaders and teachers by the example we set and decisions we make.

When we stand up for what's right, we're telling everyone around us that we believe in something. You've probably heard the expression, "You have to stand for something or you will fall for anything." Well, every time you assert yourself in a responsible manner you are demonstrating your independence and integrity. You're not just demanding respect, but proving you deserve it by giving it. You are teaching people how to treat you. You are showing what your boundaries are and declaring that you are not going to be led where you don't want to go. If you take this attitude a step further and stand up for a friend or broader principle, then you're making an even bolder statement. You're defending a specific cause and showing that you're not going to back down.

That cause might be a school dress policy, a problem in your neighborhood or an issue of greater public concern. Regardless, you are teaching because *someone* is watching — younger brothers and sisters or a kid down the street who really looks up to you even if you don't know it. Act accordingly.

You don't have to do anything to earn this admiration, it just happens. Younger kids naturally idolize teens. They watch what you do, imitate you and make you their role model. So, what are you going to do with all that power? Are you going to show

93

good character so they have that as an example? Will they see you shoveling snow or raking leaves, be impressed by your football gear or basketball skills, notice you studying or carrying your books to and from school? Or, will you impress them in the opposite manner by skipping classes, hanging out at the corner store, smoking weed, ignoring teachers and defying all authority?

A young man of purpose knows there is a heavy weight on his shoulders and he has no choice but to carry it high and proud. I've said throughout these pages that the road to manhood isn't easy. In addition to all that, we must accept the fact that real men are leaders, too.

Leadership isn't just about impressive titles or big decisions. It's also the little stuff. When I was young, I once grappled with something as small as giving my pen to a guy who didn't have one. I wanted to give it to him, but he was considered a geek and I didn't want the other guys to make fun of me for it. Eventually, I gave him the pen then braced for all the laughing and teasing sure to follow. And you know something? My friends were quiet (for a change). I made the right choice and the only consequence was feeling good about it.

Around this time, I discovered that good feelings are one of the rewards for making positive choices. After that, I started helping people as much as I could. I did it because I had stumbled upon a wonderful secret — helping someone else is one of the best gifts you can actually give yourself. You get so much joy from it and it sets an example for others in the process.

Once you realize that you have something special to give, even if it's just a pen, you begin to think of yourself as a pretty good guy.

From time to time, we all need to be told that we are okay. When you reach out to help an elderly woman cross the street or a child in distress, their gratitude means you're better than okay. You want to help again and again because there's something magical about it.

It's more than self-worth. It's almost like you're the lead good guy in an action film who saves the world, or at least the neighborhood. You feel encouraged to do one good deed after another. You find yourself opening doors or carrying groceries for someone who needs a hand. After a while this behavior becomes a natural part of your character. You think about making something of yourself and accepting challenges you may have turned down in the past. You're not afraid to run for student council, try out for the school play, get more involved in after-school activities or take tougher classes. You don't mind extra responsibilities because that's what action heroes do.

In the 7th or 8th grade, I was determined to improve my penmanship. I looked at signatures of famous people and played with my own for the next two or three years. One day, a classmate accused me of thinking I was important. He said it was stupid for trying to make my signature look fancy. I ignored him because I didn't agree. I felt a nice signature would help me develop a strong identity. And, yes, I did want to be important. I wanted to go somewhere in life. I didn't want to stay in the same old neighborhood, moping and regretful. I was a dreamer and a doer.

I now realize that most people with goals are picked on and called names. Just behave as if you were born to do something amazing, because you were. Some will call you crazy or arrogant. Every successful person I've ever known has heard that. Someone has pointed to them and said, "That person thinks they are better than everyone else." Or maybe *they* think you're better than everyone else.

I remember a teacher approaching me once and asking, "Why do you walk like you think you own this place?" I was just an eighth grader and had no idea what he was talking about. But, I decided not to let his insult affect me — and neither should you. If someone is threatened by your confidence and ambition, don't worry about it. Use it in a powerful way for good, to accomplish things, to inspire and to be the best you can.

I don't believe great leaders are anointed or elected. They have to work at it by exhibiting strength, tenacity and a genuine desire to help everyone around them do better. You prepare by conditioning yourself — practicing new skills that eventually become part of your real character.

Carry yourself a certain way. Be proud of who you are. Be polite. Don't hate, it's painful and wastes too much energy. Believe in people, it gives you permission to be tolerant. Learn to say "I love you." It's easier than you think.

Look up the meaning of big or unfamiliar words and add them to your vocabulary. When you meet new people, make it a point to remember their names. Make eye contact. Never shake hands like you're not interested. Have a strong, firm handshake that reflects your enthusiasm and inner strength. And always live by the Golden Rule: Do unto others as you would have others do unto you.

I learned all of the above before I graduated from high school. It gave me a sense of purpose and made me comfortable in my own skin. Back then, my family was Jehovah's Witness and we all had to knock on doors to share information about our faith. As a teen, I sometimes went out alone. That took courage. I matured a lot because of it. I also learned rejection at an early age and, as a result, developed incredible confidence that might pass for "swag" nowadays.

If this sounds like you, then make sure you stay on the right path. Don't believe in yourself so much that you go off the deep end like the cocky young football player who went to jail for it. A bunch of kids were standing around watching and he got caught up in the moment. In that way, he's just like any of the misguided teens I knew when I was young. Instead of chasing a dream, they spent all their time going against the system. Instead of becoming leaders, they became troublemakers.

Have you heard the saying, "To whom much is given, much is expected?" A lot is expected from you, but it doesn't amount to anything if you don't expect it of yourself. Sometimes, the best motivator is a smart girlfriend. A woman who is a leader understands the importance of strong men and will help you become a leader, too. Some young men actually do better in high school and college if they are dating an intelligent, determined young lady who shares a vision of more for herself and you. If she is going places and has good values, the young man worthy of her affections will follow suit.

An old college buddy is a good example of this. A loyal friend, he was smart but not all that excited about college. Then, he met a wonderful girl. After that, it seemed like every time I saw him he was in the library. Later, his girlfriend made the dean's list, so he made the dean's list, too. She pulled him right along, which is what happens when you're open to it.

TV Judge Greg Mathis is another example. He was a former gang member in Detroit who decided to turn his life around and go back to school. Once he received his GED and started college, however, the academic world was a bit foreign to him — until he befriended a young female honor student. It works like a charm every time. Get in a relationship with great expectations and watch the positive changes happen.

With my own wife, it was always understood that there were certain habits she would not tolerate. She thought smoking was terrible, for example, so I avoided it. Who knows what I might have gotten into if she had not been so consistently assertive. Or, look all the way up to President Barack Obama, First Lady Michelle Obama is a classic example of the strong, powerful woman beneath the wings of a strong, powerful leader. He seldom misses an opportunity to acknowledge that he wouldn't have gotten as far without her.

Just as the wrong person can bring out the worst in us, the right partner can also bring out qualities that we didn't even know we had. So, choose wisely. The girl by your side is not someone to take lightly — regardless of what some of your music might tell you. Respect members of the opposite sex. Your role is to lead, not abuse them. Uplift, comfort and, one day, provide for the right young lady. Dating eventually leads to marriage, which means you need to start out with character. Is she kind? Does she have goals? Does she insist on excellence? Is she someone you would be proud to call your wife? Will she make a good partner for raising great children.

I'm not saying that you should be preparing for marriage right now. However, I do realize that at your age you're probably developing real and powerful feelings about the opposite sex. That means you need to know how to relate to females properly. No doubt, your attempts to interact with them have led to some awkward and even embarrassing moments. Meanwhile, your friends are probably pressuring you into sexual exploration or telling you "everyone is doing it." The media isn't helping matters either. Every time you turn on the TV, go to movies, or listen to music, you are being bombarded with sexual messages. If you're lucky, there are a couple of adults in your life who can advise you or simply listen. More than likely, those adults won't be your parents. In fact, they might be tongue-tied and uncomfortable discussing sex with their son or facing the fact that he is, indeed, growing up. So what do you do? How do you make good decisions about sex and intimacy with girls?

You can navigate your sexual awakening successfully if you learn to relate to girls as people, not sexual objects. Don't use and exploit them for your sexual pleasure. If you do, you take many risks: unwanted pregnancy, sexually transmitted diseases, charges of sexual violence and harassment, and emotional pain. If a pregnancy occurs and you try to become a responsible father at such a young age, other great dreams and goals will likely go out the window for both you and the mother. Even worse, if you become an absentee father, you shift your parenting responsibilities to others, create a burden to society and harm the child.

Developing genuine and positive friendships with girls can be a wonderful experience and a great preparation for adulthood. Harness your sexual desires and learn to relate to girls with respect and real interest. Be courteous, mind your manners, give them compliments, pay attention to them and protect their reputation.

Then, someday, you will meet that special one and this practice for adulthood will bear fruit. You will enter into a committed, long-term relationship in which sex will be a beautiful, wonderful and wholesome experience. This is far different than the cheap and risky imitation of promiscuous teen sex outside of a committed relationship.

Every step you make right now is shaping your tomorrow. I have already taken this trip and can tell you that it's definitely worth steering clear of all those who would lure you down the wrong road. Today, young men are being misdirected by an onslaught of media images and messages that tear down rather than build up a legacy of responsible leadership. Don't fall into the negative traps you see on TV or hear in certain rap songs. Avoid them by building a platform of strength and excellence to stand upon. If you don't have such a platform yet, try this:

CHARACTER

Character is who you are and the base upon which every other part of your personality is built. It is the skeleton of your being; your strength, beliefs, practices and personality all stem from character. The word comes from the Greek term *charakter* meaning "engraved mark" or "symbol or imprint on the soul." It refers to the sum of traits possessed by a person, especially the moral qualities that shape our perspectives and behaviors. These qualities distinguish us from others and validate us as unique. The personal features of someone with strong character include morality, honesty, integrity, compassion and commitment. What we do and how we do it are all determined by our character.

COMMITMENT

Commitment is extremely important. Whether it's dedication to self, others or a worthy cause, it is a strong basis of moral leadership. Commitment to the right thing prevents you from wandering aimlessly through life. It starts with self and progresses toward something greater like family and community.

Committing to something means that it matters enough to warrant your time, energy, resources and efforts. It might be volunteer work, support for another individual or personal donation to a national issue. Unselfish commitment is of value even if it's the simplest of acts — keeping your word, finishing a work assignment or rolling up your sleeves to clean a local park. It means you have started a journey that *must* be completed. When you begin, zero in on a goal and path by which you plan to reach that destination. Focus, invest your mental and physical energy, and believe in the desired outcome.

PATIENCE

Life has a pace all its own even if in our eyes it sometimes moves too fast or slow. The reality is that we must be confident and trusting enough to be patient with each other, any obstacles and ourselves. We must not be so demanding that we don't give ourselves time to grow into productivity. That's like expecting an apple tree to bear fruit before its time. Life must be nurtured with the necessary ingredients before harvesting the rewards. Shaking the tree won't make it more productive; you must invest more into it first.

We live in an *instant* age of microwaves, endless television and radio channels, social media and real-time delivery of information from infinite sources. We want it all and we want it now. But, that is still not how life itself works. Outcomes result from effort and the patience we employ to see it to fruition.

PASSION

Passion is the fire that fuels our lives. It is the drive that gets our hearts beating, our lungs breathing and our minds racing. Having passion first for life and then for a cause makes it all the more worthwhile. It is also yet another rung up on the ladder of leadership. Firing up your performance sets a standard others will imitate. It shows that excellence is the only option and you are capable of leading all the way.

Passion is something that you love and respect so much it is essential to your very life and livelihood. What do you love? What matters most? What do you want to do and why? These are the factors that power our journey. It is the difference between a job and a career, a pal and a friend, a life and a love. Those who are passionate about something tend to excel at it because they're driven by want rather than need, and desire always outweighs being forced to do something.

PERSEVERANCE

Life is tough, but you are tougher if you just persevere. This characteristic will see you through tough times and get you to your goal. It is the tenacity and strength to never throw in the towel or call it a day before the job is truly done — meaning, correctly. Tough times are a test of your willingness and ability to be greater than any challenge. Like a runner who gets stronger with practice, building his endurance and strength with every lap, so will you with every obstacle or potential setback. Each challenge you overcome is yet another rung on your leadership ladder to personal and professional success.

NOW TAKE UP THE TORCH AND RUN

There you have it, the recipe for a strong person of good moral fiber who is dedicated to his manhood and mission. Apply these ingredients of good leadership and you will succeed. There will be a burning drive within you that is so fierce no one can cool it down or turn it off. That's the flame of leadership. It begins in your heart, travels to your soul and takes over your mind. It doesn't matter who ignites this flame — yourself, a girlfriend, parent, teacher, friend or role model. All that matters is that you pick up the torch and run with it.

I am but the elder who is passing it on, waving, cheering and wearing a big smile. I've done my best to lead the way, but now it is up to you. I know it's in good hands and you're more than capable of taking it from here.

FINAL THOUGHT

Witnessing the wonder of my daughter's birth inspired me to write her a love lyric that I titled simply *A Poem for Payton*. Today, she's a young teen, on the cusp of womanhood, and I feel compelled to write again—only this time not to her, but, rather, to the young man who one day soon will endeavor to court her.

Instead, I am going to simply gift Payton's future suitor with this book, throughout which Dr. Curtis Ivery liberally shares pearls of wisdom to help dawdling boys become precocious men. Indeed, if Ivery was a basketball player, he'd undoubtedly be a point guard because he drops dimes in every paragraph of *Don't Give Up, Don't Give In*.

Simply put, the tome is a clarion call to developing boys for discipline, which is crucial to success in whatever one endeavors. It is a paternal appeal to them to satiate, right now, their tender lives with yearning to go above and beyond the ordinary.

It's an entreaty for education—the almighty equalizer. On page after page, in chapter after chapter, Ivery heartens young men to learn more so they can earnestly participate in this increasingly competitive world and global economy.

Ivery's work is a request for boys to develop resolve, conjuring this excerpt from Rudyard Kipling's classic *If* about the importance of dogged determination:

> *"If you can force your heart and nerve and sinew ...*
> *To serve your turn long after they are gone,*
> *And so hold on when there's nothing in you,*
> *Except the WILL which says to them: HOLD ON!*

The book pitches service, imploring boys to be charitable and use their talents to commit to causes larger than themselves, recognizing that doing so breeds empathy—a quality of character that helps young men understand that their obligations extend beyond people who look like them and live in their neighborhoods. It beckons boys to be bold, summoning the words of that great American Robert F. Kennedy, who said, "The world demands a predominance of courage over timidity, (an) appetite for adventure over the love of ease."

Ivery also urges unity among young men and reminds them to remember, always, that they stand on the shoulders and sacrifices of a lot of people. Not just luminaries like Rosa Parks, Thurgood Marshall, Medgar Evers, and Cesar Chavez, but everyday heroes like their parents, grandparents, aunts, uncles, and community elders, too.

Lastly, Ivery admonishes boys to nurture their spirit and be obedient to their conscience, recognizing that is God talking.

Given the myriad pressures facing young men today, the book is timely, to say the least.

Without a doubt, young man, it is your life. Build it ... especially if you plan on ringing Payton's doorbell!

Kenneth A. Cole
Columnist

AFTERWORD

The voice of a seasoned leader can be quiet, dignified, bold, inspiring, demanding, angry and impatient or a combination of several expressions. But underneath its variety, a deeper, more personal voice informs all the others. It is a powerful voice that grows from the leader's unique identity, life pattern, core values and broad experience. Such is the voice of the author in this insightful offering for young men.

Dr. Curtis L. Ivery is a product of the Civil Rights Era. He grew up in the southern state of Texas, was nurtured by loving parents and began to blaze trails early. His resume is filled with examples of his trail-blazing exploits where he was the first African American to take on tasks where his voice was heard.

This distinguished leader, who happens to be one of my earliest protégés, loves to read and write. The words and ideas that appear in this book, Dr. Ivery's tenth, grow from his personal generative efforts. I would describe him as the quintessential servant-leader, who deeply feels that he has been "called" to be of service to others.

It pains him to see and read about the countless examples of young men who "miss the mark" and follow a path of poor decisions, bad choices and misguided actions, all of which lead to a less than worthwhile life.

Where can those young men turn to be given caring advice on how best to go through this experiment and experience called "life?" This little book, *Young Man, It's Your Life – Build It*, has the purpose of giving young men a literal tool box of simple steps to take that can help them to construct a meaningful life.

As I read this manuscript, these words of Ralph Waldo Emerson came into my consciousness: "What lies beneath us and what lies before us are tiny matters compared to what lies within us." Without the sense of caring, there can be no sense of community. A deep sense of caring is reflected in each of the ten chapters in his book.

The following are just some of the lessons that Dr. Ivery passes on to young men:

- Believe in yourself.
- Don't give up and don't give in.
- Keep on trying.
- Quitters never win and winners never quit.
- Take control of your own destiny.
- You are a unique creation. Nothing can replace you.
- Practice makes perfect.
- Zero in on your target and go for it.
- Love yourself first and most.
- Set goals and work to make them happen.

This book is a wonderful companion to one of Dr. Ivery's earliest works — *Journeys to Conscience: Words, Wisdom and Wit from the Voice and Pen*. These words of the author resonate throughout this book: "It is time to follow the dictates of our conscience... we need the enriching gifts of the broad spectrum of our life experience to be shared with others."

Young men and those who have a penchant for uplifting them will find value in this offering by Dr. Curtis L. Ivery.

Dr. Wright L. Lassiter, Jr.
Chancellor Emeritus
Dallas County Community College District

CIL

CPSIA information can be obtained
at www.ICGtesting.com
Printed in the USA
LVOW04*0036270116
471580LV00003B/6/P